String
Theories

Production & Art Direction: Saeah Wood
Editing: Jana Eidse & Amy Reed
Design & Layout: Ivica Jandrijević

Paperback 978-1-955671-15-6
E-Book 978-1-955671-26-2
Audiobook 978-1-955671-27-9

otterpine.com

String Theories

TIPS, CHALLENGES, AND REFLECTIONS FOR THE LIFELONG GUITARIST

ADAM LEVY AND ETHAN SHERMAN

TABLE OF CONTENTS

▶ Part I: TIPS

▶ Part II: CHALLENGES

▶ Part III: REFLECTIONS

INTRODUCTION

▶ How this book works

String Theories is a book of practice strategies for the modern guitarist who is interested in staying inspired and leveling up their playing. Everything in here has been applicable in our own working and creative lives as guitar players. Because these strategies have worked for us, we felt they'd be worth sharing with you, too.

The book is divided into three distinct sections: *Tips*, *Challenges*, and *Reflections*. *Tips* are the chapters you can breeze through in one practice session, be it five minutes or 50 minutes, to bring a fresh perspective to your next gig, jam, or recording session. *Challenges* are somewhat longer-term workouts, things that may take more time to integrate into your playing. *Reflections* are concepts to ponder, projects to continually revisit over time, real-life experiences we've had as players, and various listening and reading recommendations. At the bottom of all of the Tips and some of the Challenges, we've offered *Things to Do*—ways to apply the material to your practice over varying periods of time, specific tasks you can do today, this month, or this year. You can pick and choose from these prompts to create a rich and challenging practice that helps you meet your own musical goals.

We've tried to keep written notation to a minimum, both to encourage the reader to seek out musical references on their own and to reduce barriers for readers who are less familiar with reading music. However, some of the material in this book assumes a prerequisite of some musical knowledge. If you feel like you're in over your head, here are some recommendations to help get you up to speed:

- *A Modern Method for Guitar*, William Leavitt
- *Music Theory for Guitarists*, Tom Kolb
- *Time Awareness for All Musicians*, Peter Erskine

This book is written in a collective voice, with occasional asides from each of us when we have a personal anecdote to add. Much of the material is adapted from Adam's popular YouTube series *Guitar Tips*, expanded and formatted for the page, and there's brand-new content from both of us as well.

PART I: TIPS

As the song from Adam's YouTube series goes, *"Guitar Tips, Guitar Tips, just the Tips, just for you... Guitar Tips."* The aim of this section is to give you a concrete musical activity to work on right now, this very second, guitar in hand. Most of these are short and digestible, designed to be taken with you to whatever you're doing musically after you've completed working through the tip—more practicing, a rehearsal, a recording session, or a gig. Make sure to check out the "Things to Do" at the end of each tip for even more specificity. Get pickin'!

CHAPTER 1:

PRACTICE MAKES MUSIC

TIP: Warm Up Your Ears and Your Hands

If you practice a lot, you might already have a warm-up routine—something you do at the start of your practice time that gets your hands acclimated to the instrument, gets the blood circulating, and stretches you out a little bit. This is particularly helpful if you're planning to practice for a long while or to challenge yourself technically in any way. There are lots of resources on warming up the hands, but we need to warm up our ears, too.

ADAM: *I was talking about warm-ups with my friend Ken Rosser, who's a great guitar player in Los Angeles. He mentioned a 12-bar blues warm-up that he sometimes does at the start of a practice session to warm up his ears and hands at the same time. I tried it myself and found it to be valuable, fun, and interesting.*

▶ Ken's warm-up

Play a 12-bar blues progression, unaccompanied, to a metronome at a slow-medium tempo. In each measure, only play whole notes, but two notes simultaneously (a.k.a. *dyads*).

Things to listen for:

• **MELODY** – Listen to the top notes as a melody and the bottom notes as a secondary melody/accompaniment.

- **HARMONY** – How do the notes you're playing relate to the chords that are (invisibly) happening behind you?

As we do this, our fingers are moving very slowly (whole notes!), and our ears can tune into the separate notes and their movement. When you play a big chord right off the bat, it's harder to hear the distinct notes than to hear the chord as a big chunk of sound. We want to have two notes and hear them both clearly.

Don't simply count through the four beats and *then* think of where you're going next. While all the notes are ringing out, you can listen ahead to where you want to go. Follow your ears. As the two notes are ringing, get hungry for something new to happen, and then feed that hunger by going there (or staying there...that might make you hungrier).

This is a way to make music where you're thinking about the guitar in a melodic and contrapuntal way; "contrapuntal" refers to the relationship between two independent melodic lines. This can pay off over time, opening up possibilities on the guitar that you wouldn't get to if you were playing familiar chord shapes all the time. It warms up your hands and strengthens the connection between them and your inner ear.

THINGS TO DO

TODAY Do this exercise.

THIS MONTH Do this exercise in a new key daily. Given that there are 30 days in a month and 12 keys, you'll hit each key at least twice, and some three times. You could rotate through the keys chromatically, or by the circle of 4ths/5ths. Keep a record in your practice journal of which key you warmed up in on a given day.

THIS YEAR Do this exercise every day, but in a new key every month. Spending 30-odd days in the same key will give you an opportunity to *really* get to know it.

TIP: Practice Making Real Music

There is always going to be technical material that you can work on. As soon as you can, try to put it into music. For example, if you're working on barre chords, practice them in a song. Perhaps you'll choose a song that's not entirely made up of barre chords but includes one or two. Or, take a song you like to play, and work it out using only barre chords.

Another option is to create that musical context yourself. Write a song or short étude that puts into practice the technical skill you're trying to improve. An étude is a short piece of music aimed to improve a particular instrumental technique. It doesn't have to be a long-winded magnum opus. Even something four or eight measures long can still be a song.

ADAM: *When I studied with Ted Greene, I noticed that he was never into doing strictly technical stuff for the sake of it. As much as he could do amazing stretches with his hands, when people asked if they should do exercises to improve their finger reach, he'd always say, "Don't practice that—that's not music." Instead, he'd write a tune or an arrangement integrating big reaches, as a way to make music out of all the hard work.*

At the end of the day, technique is on you. You do have to take care of technique in order to achieve what you want to on the instrument, but if you're going to work as a guitar player, people will be interested in you for your musicality, not your technique. So, if you're practicing a lot of technical exercises, make sure that you're balancing them with real music.

THINGS TO DO

TODAY Pick one song you know well and apply whatever technical challenges you're working on to its form.

THIS MONTH Make a list of four songs you'd like to learn. Spend a week on each song. For the first half of the week, learn the song using techniques you're comfortable with. In the second half of the week, apply new technical challenges to the form of the song.

THIS YEAR Make a list of playing techniques (no more than 12) that you'd like to be more fluent in than you currently are. Spend one month on each, alternating their application between songs you know well and songs you're learning.

TIP: Form Follows Function

There's no one "correct" technique for the guitar. How you hold your pick (or your plucking fingers), where you place your thumb on the back side of the neck, and so on—these are personal choices, which should always be directed by two questions: *What are you trying to achieve musically? What's the most efficient and effective way of achieving the thing you're trying to do?*

Every aspect of your left-hand and right-hand technique should be in the service of your musical goals. Here's a real-life example:

 ADAM: *A student came to me and said, "I watch a lot of other guitarists play. They've got all this power in their right hand. I feel like I'm doing all the right things, but I can't find the power I want to get."*

I thought it could be a timing thing. A steady groove can be a powerful engine behind a big sound. I turned on the metronome and found that my student's strumming was in perfect time, so I continued to watch her play. Finally, I saw what the issue was. As she strummed, the tip of the pick was pointed up toward her face about 15–20 degrees, instead of being parallel to the floor. That was enough to dissipate the energy of her strum. By rotating her wrist so that the pick was once again parallel to the floor, there was suddenly much more volume and clarity in her sound.

TIP: Keep a Practice Journal

It's worth keeping notes on the various short-term and long-term projects that you're spending practice time on. Be specific in your journal entries. Which pieces of music are you working on? What tempo are you practicing at? Which keys are you practicing in? Write it all down.

You may not be working on a particular piece of music today. It could be raw material, like scales, arpeggios, chord forms, or something else. Whatever it is you're spending practice time on, find a way to log what it is, where you're at with it, and any thoughts or feelings that you have around the material.

Here are some questions you can ask yourself:

- Which parts of this music or material are giving you trouble, and what parts are coming more easily?
- What are your short-term and long-term goals in working this music or material?
- Where are you trying to get to in your practice, and how does this piece or material fit into that?
- What's exciting to you about this music or material?

In a perfect world, we would practice every day and always be wonderfully in the flow. What tends to happen in real life is we'll miss a day (or two, or three) and lose track of where we were. That's where a practice journal can really come in handy—all you have to do is open it up to your last entry. It's a practical guide to help keep your practice moving forward. It can also help you when you're feeling frustrated that you're not improving.

ETHAN: *When I was about 18, I had the opportunity to attend a workshop led by Robert Fripp. I voiced frustration that it didn't feel like I was improving. He responded that, in his experience (I'm paraphrasing), the greatest improvements in his playing never felt like improvements when they were actually happening. Something to consider when you hit what feels like a roadblock.*

Look back a few weeks, months, or even the whole year, and see where you were then. We'll bet you're a lot farther along than you think you are. So, take a moment to appreciate the fact that if you keep practicing, you *will* keep getting better. That is no small thing.

▶ Tips for maintaining a practice journal:

- Any notebook will do. Any pen will do. Don't overthink the tools.
- Include all the details: the day of the week, the date, the time, the place, your mood, the guitar.
- Be clear and specific in your notes. Avoid shorthand.
- When you take a day off and don't practice, write that in your journal.
- Be honest. This journal is just for you, so there's no reason to oversell or undersell.

ONE DAY OF ETHAN'S PRACTICE JOURNAL

→ *Played through fugue from J.S. Bach's "Lute Suite #2," along with Julian Bream's recording, slowed down to 50%. Sometimes*

I get distracted or startled by the differences between fingerings (sometimes he'll voice a line in a different octave than I learned it, to name one example), as I initially learned this piece from a book with specific fingerings, sporadically referring to recordings. I learned my lesson. When I feel ready to move on to the next movement in this lute suite, I'll use an even combination of recorded and notated sources to help commit it to memory in a musical way.

→ Mr. Goodchord, Vol. 1 *(Goodrick):*

→ *Open-voiced triads, bass note low E, cycle 4, keys C, F, G, A♭, D♭, G♭.*

→ *Open-voiced triads, bass note A, cycle 4, keys A, D, E, B, B♭, E♭.*

→ Sight-Reading for the Contemporary Guitarist *(Dempsey): harmonic reading exercises in B, page 73.*

→ Advanced Reading Studies *(Leavitt): harmonic reading only, pages 27–29 (9th position).*

→ *Learned "Harbor Lights" from Elvis Presley's recording.*

ONE DAY OF ADAM'S PRACTICE JOURNAL

→ *Warm-up time, 10 minutes, using* Approaching the Guitar *(Bertoncini).*

→ *Horizontal Chromatic Studies, pages 4–5.*

→ *Eighth notes, eighth-note triplets, and sixteenth notes, 40–60 bpm.*

→ *Harmonic major scales (1, 2, 3, 4, 5, b6, 7), 30 minutes.*

→ *Keys: F major, B major.*

→ *Four-fret positions, 1st–12th.*

→ *Eighth notes, 60 bpm.*

→ *This scale sounds so odd to me still, but I'm trying to own it.*

→ *Progressions Derived from Triad Chord Streams (Ted Greene study), 10 minutes.*

→ *60–72 bpm.*

→ *Not easy because of so much lateral and diagonal movement, but it sounds beautiful when it starts to flow.*

→ *Sketched a chord-melody arrangement of "Over the Rainbow," based on original sheet music, 20 minutes.*

→ *Key: E♭*

→ *Some drop-2 voicings, some triads, moving voices inside the chords.*

→ *Really unusual harmony in the original bridge!*

THINGS TO DO

TODAY Buy a notebook and a pen. Practice, then put it all in your journal.

THIS MONTH Rinse and repeat.

THIS YEAR Keep it up! At the end of this year, go back and read through some of your journal entries.

TIP: A Sample One-Hour Practice Routine

When students ask us about practicing, two issues frequently come up. *What* to practice, and *how* to practice.

Many of us also have limited time to practice—one hour per day may be all we can do. So, here's a template for a one-hour practice routine. You can fill in the *what* with all kinds of different stuff, depending on what you're working on in any given season of practice. This routine has three active segments, two resting segments, and one reflective segment.

▶ One-hour practice routine

FIFTEEN MINUTES: TECHNIQUE

This could be a scale fingering, an arpeggio fingering, or a little exercise from a book. It could even be an excerpt of a piece of music that presents specific technical challenges. Don't worry about playing anything from beginning to end, just little movements. Spend some of this time using a metronome.

FIVE MINUTES: BREAK

Put your guitar down and let your mind go away from music for five minutes. Don't consciously think about what you've just been doing. You'll still be processing everything you've just worked on at a subconscious level.

FIFTEEN MINUTES: MUSIC

Work on a composed piece or song that has a clear beginning, middle, and ending. The goal here is to be musical and to work up a piece of music, ultimately to a level where you could perform it. Spend some time with the metronome, spend some time without it. Break difficult sections into easy-to-digest bits, then slowly string them together.

FIVE MINUTES: BREAK

Take a real honest-to-goodness break. Try not to check your phone or anything like that. If you've been sitting, definitely stand up and move around. Maybe take a quick walk around the block.

FIFTEEN MINUTES: CREATIVE TIME

Improvise, in any style. If improvising isn't your thing, you could use this time for composing or producing. It's great if you're creating something that utilizes some of the stuff you've been working on earlier in this hour, musically or technically.

Over time, anything you're working on technically will seep into your creative side, so you don't have to force it. In any case, whatever gets your creative juices going is the right thing. If giving yourself an assignment with limits or a framework suits your temperament, go for it. Other people seem to do better at this point in practicing if it's wide-open, free play.

FIVE MINUTES: JOURNAL

Use this time to reflect. Write down the things you practiced. If you used a metronome, mark down the tempos you played at. If you're playing composed pieces, write down the measures or sections you played. Be specific. You can also note how your practice time felt—gratifying, frustrating, whatever.

That's the hour.

If you've got more than one hour to practice in a day, that's amazing! After an hour, I'd take a longer break, 15-20 minutes or longer, doing something else entirely. If you have another full hour later in the day, you could repeat this template.

Another way to spend a second hour would be to sit and listen to music mindfully—that's another kind of practice altogether. Not merely having music playing in the background as you do at other times, but a session of hyper-focused listening. Make a playlist for yourself that you want to feed into your ears, brain, and heart, and spend some quality time with that music.

This is how we practice, and this is how we recommend our students practice. Try it out, and see what happens.

CHAPTER 2:

REFINE YOUR SENSE OF TIME AND PLACE

TIP: Get Into the Groove

When a guitar player who primarily works in the melodic realm—soloing, improvising, jamming—has to, for the first time, play something that sits and settles rhythmically, there are some challenges that come into play. For example, finding the right placement of the part within the beat, consistency of that rhythmic placement, note length, dynamics, and how it all relates to the rest of the band (if there is a band).

Just playing the right notes in the right order isn't grooving. The good news is, grooving isn't one of those "you have it or you don't" talents. It's a musical skill that can be honed like any other.

Here are a couple of rhythm guitar concepts that you can run with and work on. Examples are not included here because we want you to be creative and come up with your own!

1. **Jazz: Walking a bass line with chords on top**
   For two measures, improvise a quarter-note bass line on one or both of the bottom two strings while playing a static chord on the upper strings. Ninth chords work well—i.e., maj9, 7(#9), 7(9), and min9.

   The bass line should be consistently locked up with that quarter note, and the upper voices of the chord should be moving independently, not adjusting to whatever the bass is doing. The way the separate parts coexist together is what creates the groove.

2. R&B/Funk: Meters-esque range switching

The Meters were an instrumental funk band from New Orleans that grooved like mad. The guitar player, Leo Nocentelli, often played parts that would move between registers fairly quickly.

Again, two measures are enough to work with. Improvise a single-note bass line on the lower strings for the first bar, and then play some syncopated chord stabs on the upper strings (preferably between frets 5–14) in the second bar.

Play both of these exercises with your metronome set to at least 80 BPM. Record yourself (into a looper, if you're able). Once you've got it playing back, try to jam along with it. Does it feel good? Does the bass line make you want to move? Do the chords sit in a comfy place with the bass line, or are they herky-jerky?

The bass line and chords may not necessarily sit on the beat in the same way. Bass lines tend to be right on the beat, or slightly ahead, while the placement of the chords often depends on the context of the song being played and the feel that it calls for.

It's good to experiment with different placements for each part. See what feels good to you, both while playing it and while listening back and jamming along. Sometimes what feels good to us in the moment doesn't sound very good, and sometimes things that end up sounding great feel quite unnatural at first.

▶ Beat placement variations:

- Bass ahead/chords back
- Bass back/chords ahead

• Both early
• Both late

It's important to tune into the relativity of musical time. If you don't become familiar with this theory, you may find yourself playing on one side of the beat all the time—and you'll be missing a critical aspect of music that's very real and happening all the time.

If you listen to Chuck Berry's original "Johnny B. Goode," you'll hear a great example of this. The band isn't dividing up the time the same way. Berry and the bass player and the drummer are all articulating their own concept of eighth notes slightly differently—and there's beautiful sonic tension in that disagreement. This is subtle, but once you become aware of how to use it in your own music it can be a useful tool to mix up how you play with others in different styles.

Experiment with dynamic variations as well. See if you can make the bass line loud but the chord quiet, and vice versa. Any number of parameters can be switched around. Get creative!

THINGS TO DO

TODAY Pick one of the above approaches and spend 10–20 minutes working on it.

THIS MONTH Do it regularly. When you practice, record yourself, listen back, and take note of your rhythmic tendencies. When do you hear yourself pushing or pulling, rushing or dragging? How does it feel when you're dead on? Compare how you sound after the fact to how it feels in the moment. Can you close the gap?

THIS YEAR Write ten songs or études that feature one or both of these rhythmic concepts. They can be wholly original compositions or a rhythmic contrafact—a tune where the rhythm is lifted from an existing piece of music—but the melodic and harmonic content are yours.

TIP: Befriend Your Metronome

A person's time feel is directly proportionate to how comfortable they feel with what they're playing. If you know a song super well, then your time feel will usually be solid. If you are unsure about some aspect of it, the pure anxiety of that will cause the time feel to suffer.

The main thing that playing with a metronome does for us is give us a point of reference for our time. It also helps us focus. (Note: A metronome does not make you groove, and a metronome does not make you swing.)

Human nature is to both rush and drag, in micro and macro variations. Playing with a metronome can help us find out where we tend to rush and drag within a piece of music or an improvisation. The following metronome workouts can be applied to anything you're working on.

▸ Metronome workouts:

- Set the metronome to click on every beat of the time signature you're playing in.
- Set the metronome to click on beats two and four. This can help you comfortably play music with a "swing eighths" feel.
- One click per bar. This can be placed anywhere along the eighth-note continuum (on any numbered beat, or any *-and*, as in *1-and-2-and*).
- One click every two bars. Same as above.

- One click every four, eight, or sixteen bars. Same as above.
- Deliberately force yourself to speed up and slow down within any given phrase, but try to land back on the click. Test yourself: know how much you've displaced the time. This helps train us to be both fluid and precise at the same time.
- Set the metronome to play exclusively on upbeats. This seems especially helpful for bebop-style melodies and lines and for playing with drummers or percussionists who play a lot of upbeats.
- Set the metronome for every eighth note. I find this useful at the beginning of learning a fast line with complicated fingering. It helps to slow down and consider every move you need to make. When I'm playing at this slow a speed, I will play a passage only once or twice before increasing the tempo—it can be tempting to get stuck here.

Becoming comfortable with these metronome exercises isn't necessarily a linear process or a list you need to check off. I encourage you to mix, match, and explore. Find out if you have any particular tendencies. Do you slow down when playing spaced out phrases if the click hits once per four bars on the -and of beat three? I'm sure I do!

It's not about having "perfect" time. A lot of the recorded music we all love, made over the past 100 years, fluctuates in tempo all over the place. It's more about refining and trusting your own internal clock so that you feel the pulse and form of the music deeply, regardless of whatever rhythmic information another musician might throw at you.

THINGS TO DO

TODAY Get a metronome. The quickest way is to download an app on your phone, but a stand-alone analog or digital one will give your practice space a little more *vibe*, and Instagram won't beckon. Now turn it on—100 BPM is a good starting point—and just play something along with it. It doesn't matter what. A song, an improvisation...it's all good. As you play, see how long your internal quarter note can be the same as the metronome's. Record yourself, and listen back. When do you start to drift away? Why?

THIS MONTH Every time you practice, whether it's music you know or new music you're learning, spend 25-50% of your practice time with the metronome on. Pick one or two of the workouts listed and get it feeling good at a clean tempo.

THIS YEAR Listen to records and tap time along with them using any and all of the above workouts, as if *you* were the metronome.

TIP: Always Have an Exit Strategy

Guitar players have a bit of a reputation for playing the musical equivalent of run-on sentences. It's true, to a certain extent. If you play a wind instrument like trumpet or saxophone, you have to breathe, so a rambling musical line doesn't happen as much. Playing a horn makes you much more aware of phrasing with your breath, much like a singer would. Guitarists make our music with our fingers, so we don't have as much of a physical impetus to stop. The following is an exercise to work on *not* rambling on, but finishing your phrases.

▸ Practice finding your ending:

- Improvise two-bar phrases in 4/4 time, and pick a specific rhythmic spot where your phrase will end every time, no matter what. Visualize plotting a data point along a graph.

  Don't worry about how you start, and don't worry about what happens in the middle. But whatever you do, don't cross your end point. This is something worth doing without any accompaniment.
- Play the phrase, and end where you decided you'll end. You can, of course, apply it to any harmonic context or tune you're working with, but this exercise is more about the rhythm than any specific note choices.
- Move around the guitar while you do this. Don't restrict yourself to any specific position.
- Once you feel comfortable with the parameters you've set, you could move your last note closer inside the bar, so that you're

ending sooner. If you tend to end phrases on the -*and* of beat four, how about ending right on beat four itself?

- Once you're sick of two-bar phrases, extend it to three-bar phrases, then four, then all the way out to eight bars, if you can hear that far ahead.
- This idea isn't limited to single-note improvised lines. You can also practice comping this way in a jazz or R&B context (think 16-note funk strumming, letting off at any point inside those 16 notes).
- The big idea here is that you're thinking about the endpoint before you even begin. Don't be like a cat caught up a tree—have a plan to get down gracefully, and finish what you started.

THINGS TO DO

TODAY Turn to the tip "Be Your Own Jam Buddy" and apply the above ideas to it.

THIS MONTH Whenever you find yourself playing with other musicians, be conscious of your phrasing as much as you can, in whatever role you're playing.

THIS YEAR Read Hal Galper's book, *Forward Motion*.

CHAPTER 3:

LEVEL UP: FRESH PERSPECTIVES ON SOME FUNDAMENTALS

TIP: Reuse, Reduce, Recycle

Any guitarist looking to level up on their instrument is inevitably confronted with the idea that they need to learn more chords, or at least more voicings for the chords they already know. This can be an overwhelming task. The guitar's harmonic universe can seem infinite, with a myriad of inversions, string sets, and fingerings available for any given set of notes. However, it doesn't have to feel like that. A simple way to maximize your skill is to make more use of the chords you already know.

▸ Reuse

You don't have to play every chord inversion imaginable to sound good or "hip." Sure, all the ways to play Cmaj7 exist, but some of them might not sound all that great to you, or they may be hard on your hands.

Luckily for us, familiar chord shapes can be repurposed for multiple harmonic contexts. Cmaj7, for example, could also function as an Am7, or an Fmaj7, depending on the root note being played under it. Make the most of what you know.

▸ Reduce

Use fewer chords, but do more with them. Did you know that inside any four-note chord voicing are 14 other voicings? There are four three-note voicings, six two-note voicings, and four more one-note voicings. *Can one note be considered a chord,* you ask? It depends. If surrounded by other music, the one note may very well imply a full chord.

Four-note and three-note voicings are really all that's necessary to make musical statements on the guitar with clarity, especially as an accompanist. If the music you're playing requires more than that, you might be better off at a piano. Instead of getting hung up on the infinitude of the things you don't know, discover the limitlessness within the things you already know.

▶ Recycle

Applying one of these shapes to a song you know well can open up new possibilities. Here's an example of a two-note scheme taken through "Softly, as in a Morning Sunrise":

Our first chord is a Cm6. In full-voiced form, it looks like this:

Figure 1.

Here's one set of two notes inside that voicing:

Figure 2.

Here's the shape of those two notes played consistently throughout an A-section of the tune:

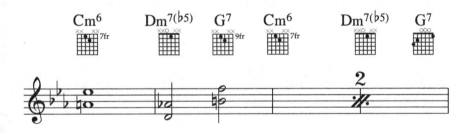

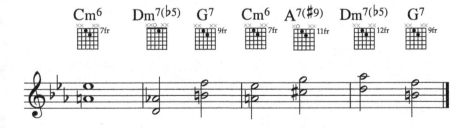

Figure 3.

THINGS TO DO

TODAY Pick a song you know and love and see how far you can take one voicing scheme through the tune, without changing the string set it's on. (Reuse.)

THIS MONTH Write a song of your own. Rather than learning ten new shapes, learn one, and see if you can find ten different ways to use it throughout the tune. (Recycle.)

THIS YEAR When playing with others, see how long you can keep something going before you change it in any way. (Reduce.)

TIP: Position Yourself

Position playing means limiting your fretting hand to a specific area of the fretboard, letting your fingers land naturally, without shifting laterally. When you're in 5th position, for example, anything that happens at the 5th fret will be played by your 1st finger, anything at the 6th fret by your 2nd finger, and so on.

Two of our favorite guitar books are Mick Goodrick's *The Advancing Guitarist* and Wayne Krantz's *An Improviser's OS*. Both cover position playing in depth, from two different perspectives.

In Goodrick's model, each position encompasses a six-fret span. From 5th position, you can reach back one fret (to the 4th fret) with your 1st finger or reach forward (to the 9th fret) with your 4th finger. This allows for complete chromaticism: you can play any note you want, from top to bottom.

Krantz's concept is more austere. In *An Improviser's OS*, 5th position is limited to the notes playable at frets 5 through 8. There, if you were to improvise in the key of E major, you'd have no C♯ in the low octave as it's out of position on both the 6th and 5th strings. Try playing a complete E major scale in this position. Which other notes (if any) are out of bounds?

THINGS TO DO

TODAY Improvise your way around a single scale in a particular position. Spend five minutes following Mick

Goodrick's way, and another following Wayne Krantz's. Try to just play. Don't think about it too much.

THIS MONTH Go buy these two books. Each is an embarrassment of riches.

THIS YEAR Work with the material in the books. Set specific goals, and journal your progress.

TIP: Outside Is Inside

How do you play "outside"? What is "outside," anyway?

To most musicians, to play outside means playing musical ideas that sound seemingly unrelated to the harmony or accompaniment behind them. It can also mean playing outside of expectations—yours, or anybody listening to you.

Playing outside is a very personal thing. One person's outside may be somebody else's inside, and vice versa. You may love the sound of it but not know where to begin.

If you're new to outside playing, a great way in is to approach it from the inside. It's not about doing a lot of calculations to figure out which notes are going to sound "weird" in any given harmonic context. Rather, you can explore fundamental elements of music in unexpected ways. By doing this, you may be outside everything around you, but you're inside something else, something you (hopefully) already know.

▶ Here are four ways to play outside, inside:

1. Inside harmony
This is most efficient (and less heady) if you stick to triad-based ideas. Play something that makes musical sense, but to some other chord that nobody else is hearing except you. For example, on an A major chord, you can play ideas that belong to

the family of B minor. It's not terribly outside but not terribly inside either.

Now what if you play inside B♭? You're not limited to one chord here. You can even set up a sequence of chords. On top of an A chord, say, you could play C minor, F♯, and B♭. This works well if you use a looper. Set up a simple one-chord vamp, and go hog wild.

2. Inside melody
Play a melodic phrase or scale sequence, and move it around so that it doesn't stay in the scale, and so it doesn't always start on the same beat. A listener will hear where you're going because the core of your idea is a simple melodic fragment that you've already established.

3. Inside rhythm
Take a short rhythmic phrase (a.k.a. *ostinato*) and play any note or chord on it. Pitch doesn't matter—the engine is the repetition of the rhythm. Once you establish that, you can change up the pitches to play single notes or chords.

4. Inside shapes
This is a more guitaristic perspective. A shape that sounds major on one string set will sound totally different on any other string set. Here, you're inside your hand. It feels the same, but because of the tuning of the guitar and the layout of the fretboard, things won't necessarily sound the same.

If you're working within any of these four elements, the mere fact that what you're playing is outside its surroundings will give you the effect you're looking for. What you play will also have its own sense of gravity because there is some internal logic at work.

▸ **Further thoughts:**

- You don't always need to know exactly *how* you're going outside. It can also just be a feeling, a mood, something intangible.
- Learn music that sounds outside to you. Analyze it as best you can. You might find that small chunks of it will actually be inside something, and it's the context of everything else that gives it the effect of sounding "out."
- Build up your ears of expectation: when you hear what you'd be expected to play next, listen also for what you can do (or are already doing) that's outside of those expectations, whether they're yours or someone else's.

▸ **Recommended reading:**

- *Perpetual Frontier: The Elements of Free Music*, Joe Morris
- *The Primacy of the Ear*, Ran Blake
- *Improvisation*, Derek Bailey

THINGS TO DO

TODAY On your next practice routine, jam session, or gig, pick one or two outside approaches from above. Make a conscious effort to shoehorn them into your playing—within musical reason, of course.

THIS MONTH Learn a passage (of any length—whatever feels manageable for you) from an "outside" piece of music of your choice. Sing along with it, and play it on your guitar.

THIS YEAR As you listen to music, listen actively with ears of expectation. When does a player do something you've come to expect them to do, and when do they buck expectations? When they play something outside the realm of what you'd expect, how do they get in and out of it?

CHAPTER 4:

LISTEN UP: THE MORE YOU HEAR, THE MORE YOU HEAR

TIP: Practice Without Your Guitar

Life can get busy, and many of us aren't able to spend an hour or more on the guitar as often as we may want to. However, that doesn't mean our musicality needs to be neglected. There are growth opportunities in front of us all the time, even when the guitar isn't.

Whether you have a lot of time, a little, or almost none, make sure you're using your time well, even if you can't get your hands on the strings.

▸ Here are three ways to practice without your guitar:

1. Internalize forms

Unless a piece of music is particularly technically complicated, you don't need an instrument to get a sense of its form. Count bars and make a mental map of each section leading to another.

If it's hard to keep straight in your mind, open a note on your phone, or get out a piece of paper, and jot down the form as it passes by. Here's an example:

- Intro — 4 bars
- Verse 1 — 12 bars
- Verse 2 — 12 bars
- Chorus — 16 bars

The mere process of doing this can help you understand a song better, regardless of whether or not you take your "cheat sheet" to the gig with you.

2. **Create melodic and harmonic memory**

Anytime you listen to music, you have an opportunity to think about the melody (any instrumental or vocal melody) and imagine how that melody would take shape on the fingerboard. What are the chords? How would you play them? Visualize the guitar inside your head.

3. **Focus on rhythm**

Improving your sense of time is super easy to do without the guitar. Tap your fingers and subdivide in your head. Eighth notes and eighth-note triplets are a great place to start. Go back and forth between the two, and see if you can feel that shift in your body, even without the guitar.

THINGS TO DO

TODAY Go for a walk and put a record in your ears. Follow along with the rhythm, melody, harmony, and form on your inner fretboard.

THIS MONTH As you go about each day, visualize yourself practicing whatever music you're currently working on. This can be a specific song or free improvisation. Do the same challenges you have with a guitar in hand happen without? If so, work through them internally.

THIS YEAR Keep it up. The clearer all the qualities of the music become in your mind, the clearer they'll be when you play your instrument—especially while improvising.

TIP: Train Your Ears

The first step to improving your inner ear is setting your goals and getting specific. What exactly do you want to achieve? The clearer you can get with that, the more goal-oriented you can be in your practice.

Every area of music can be improved by training your ear to hear it better—rhythm, harmony, and melody alike. For some people, ear training means that you want to get better at tuning the guitar without an electronic tuner or other pitch reference. Another kind of ear training would be to connect more intentionally with the music that you hear in your imagination, instead of merely hunting and pecking. Whatever it is for you, name it and claim it.

▶ Transcribe some music

In a broad sense, transcribing just means to listen to some recorded music and figure out what's going on. You can certainly write it down (that's the "scribe" in "transcribe"), but it's the actual act of figuring that immediately connects your ear to the music.

One benefit of writing stuff down is that you can come back to it later to study and analyze it, if that helps you understand it better. Start simple with things that you can play and hear. Don't start with something so far beyond your ears that it'll frustrate you in the first bar. Increase the challenge incrementally over time.

If you specifically want to figure out what a guitarist is doing, pick a recording where the guitar is more exposed in the mix—say, a solo or duo recording. That way, you can really hone in on what the guitar is doing. The more of this you do, the more adept you'll get at figuring out what the guitar is up to when there's more going on in the mix.

If you're transcribing guitar, figure out what the other instruments around it are doing too. Transcribe bass parts, piano parts, horn parts, and even drum parts. See if you can appropriate to your guitar what those other instruments are doing.

▶ Play along with records

Try to chase/echo what's being played in the moment. This is applicable to all kinds of music. Get into the groove with the rhythm section and play rhythm. If somebody's improvising or playing something melodic (or even singing), use your guitar to try and echo what they're doing. Pretend you're a delay pedal set at 300 ms—see how closely you can echo what you've just heard. No matter how good you get at doing these exercises in the practice room, you want your ear training to be done in the service of making real music with real people so that you can react to what you're hearing. Try to hear the big picture of what's going on as well as all of the individual nuances. While you listen, focus on individual nuances of each instrument being played while simultaneously listening for the big picture.

Slow ballads are fine. Three-chord songs are fine. It doesn't have to be anything particularly crazy. No matter what you do to train your ears, do a little bit every day, every single day, and it *will* get better, even if it doesn't seem like it at first.

THINGS TO DO

TODAY Take 30 minutes and transcribe something that you can sing and play along with at tempo, without having to slow it down. It doesn't matter how much you can get done in that time frame; doing the 30 minutes is enough.

THIS MONTH Make a playlist of five to eight songs you love. They can be all by the same artist or a variety. Play along with the playlist every night before you go to sleep. For extra credit, record yourself and listen back the next night before playing it again. Take stock. What can you learn about how you played yesterday that you can apply to how you play today?

THIS YEAR Pick out a longer-form piece of music to transcribe—a full solo, or a classical piece. Chip away at it regularly until you're done. Make sure to take days where you revisit what you've already learned, so that it stays fresh in your ears and hands.

TIP: Transcribe Conceptually

Often what we really want to appropriate from the musicians we love isn't their specific notes, rhythms, and phrases, but the way their playing made us feel—the musical "essence" so to speak.

However, many of us have been told that the only way to internalize a musician's essence is to learn what they play, literally note for note. While the act of literal transcription can have value, technical and otherwise, it can sometimes feel like a distraction from discovering how *you* play.

 ETHAN: *I doubt I'm alone in remembering the first time I paid attention to the guitar work of Larry Carlton. Around the time I first heard him, I was working on getting comfortable improvising through jazz-like chord changes, but for fun, I was listening mostly to rock-oriented music. My guitar teacher, probably sensing I needed to reconcile these two worlds, played me Steely Dan's "Kid Charlemagne," where Carlton is prominently featured. My jaw dropped to the floor. "What is that?" I remember thinking. "I want to do that!"*

I spent the next month or two down a Larry Carlton-as-session-guy rabbit hole, digging deep into his soloing on Steely Dan records and the way he complemented singer-songwriters like Joni Mitchell. I played along with him for hours on end, trying to imitate the nuances and inflections of his playing as closely as I could.

After a little while, I realized that although there was a lot to be learned from Carlton's playing, I could never fully duplicate what he did to my satisfaction. There were always subtleties that eluded me, and listening to my own improvising never quite evoked the same charge in me that I got when I listened to him. I eventually lost interest in trying to be Larry Carlton and moved on to another guitar hero. I can still sing the solo from "Kid Charlemagne" though.

You've probably had similar experiences throughout your own journey as a guitar player. Yet, common music-education wisdom still holds that through this process of imitation and osmosis, we somehow find our *own* voice on our instruments—a voice that is the summation of everything we've ever learned to play and every musician whose code we've cracked.

This can conjure up a mental image of a musical Frankenstein made of a bunch of unrelated pieces of player's styles, rather than one cohesive approach to making music: *What do I sound like? Well, imagine David Grier's beard, 1970s Paul McCartney's mullet, Brad Mehldau's left hand, and Vinnie Colaiuta's right foot.* Frankenstein monsters are fascinating to look at, but you probably don't want to invite one to your birthday party.

▶ The art of conceptual transcription

If you want to replicate the *feeling* of something, it doesn't make much sense to just reverse-engineer the end results of someone's music-making process so you can spit it back out verbatim. You must go deeper, reverse-engineering the process itself, and interpreting it into the musical language you're already working with. We call this *conceptual transcription.*

This of course involves *a lot* of active, focused listening, even without the guitar in your hand. You're not going to get anywhere until you've heard your chosen study subject so much that you can imagine their sound in your head without having to put a record on. Whatever knowledge you have of the fretboard and musical fundamentals will help too.

Whoever this person is for you, listen to them a lot, and as you listen, mark down timestamps on recordings where you hear a musical gesture that excites you. Then, listen to it over and over and over, until you can describe what you're hearing in something close to layman's terms (i.e., *"She hit this note, and then she hit this chord after it, and then the top note stayed the same while the chord kept getting lower, and she waited a little longer after each chord to do it again"*).

▸ Creating a personal library of gestures

It's not so important that you find the most accurate words as long as they're plain and clear. Keep metaphors and flowery language to a minimum. What's useful about this is that you're creating a personal library of musical gestures that you know you love, that are always available to you to compose and improvise with, and that aren't necessarily dependent on any tonal or rhythmic preconditions to make them work.

If what you love about a musician is the way they interact with other musicians, you can include that in your description as well (i.e., *"The guitar player did this thing and then the drummer did this other thing, and the two of them one after another made it sound like the drummer framed the edges of what the guitar player just played"*).

Once you've got some concepts verbalized, begin to apply them, one at a time, to your playing—in songs, in improvisation, while soloing, and while playing with others. Here's an example of one approach to that:

> **ADAM:** *I was thinking about conceptual transcription recently while listening to a bunch of Jesse Ed Davis's recordings. He's probably most famous for having played the guitar solo on Jackson Browne's "Doctor My Eyes"—an incredible solo that, according to legend, was done in one take. He's also featured on some of Taj Mahal's early sessions and was in the house band for George Harrison's Concert for Bangladesh.*
>
> *When I listen to Davis, I really don't know how he did it. His vocabulary was fairly standard electric blues, yet a lot of things that he did sound unfamiliar somehow. Below are some strategies I came up with to get closer to his sound.*

▶ Play in less familiar boxes

When we're talking about electric-blues vocabulary, that generally means pentatonic boxes. If we're in, say, A minor (or C major), most guitar players would start in the familiar pentatonic form at the 5th fret.

In this position, you can improvise phrases we all know and love (and maybe hate a little too). The easily bendable notes in this position, in particular, tend to lead to clichéd blues-rock phrasing (i.e., D up to E on the 3rd string; G up to A on the 2nd string; C up to D on the 3rd string). But if you want to leave people listening to your records 25 years later and scratching their heads, you may need to try something less common.

By shifting up to the next highest minor-pentatonic pattern, you'll find a different set of bends, which will lead to different sorts of phrasing (i.e., E up to F# on the 3rd string; A up to B on the 2nd string; D up to E on the 3rd string).

Davis can certainly be heard playing in the familiar blues vernacular, but some of his bends sound really different. Perhaps he was exploring other positions?

▸ Play out of another key entirely

Taking the above idea one step further, try playing the B minor pentatonic scale, at the 7th fret. It will sound loosely related to the key center of A minor (or C major) because there's some commonality in the notes. Overlaying the B minor pentatonic scale on an A blues can be a cool sound in and of itself, but we'll primarily be using it to get some different bends in an A blues context. We'll now have these available: E up to F# on the 3rd string; A up to B on the 2nd string; D up to E on the 3rd string.

Again, we don't know that Davis was thinking this way, but his playing holds enough surprises to suggest that he was exploring some less-traveled shapes on the fretboard.

THINGS TO DO

TODAY Go through the pentatonic boxes you don't know as well, and see what's there (especially with regard to bends). Find a one-chord vamp online or, better yet, make one yourself. Improvise over it in the pentatonic shapes you're least familiar with.

THIS MONTH Do your own conceptual transcription. Pick a player you love and sum up why you love them in 5–10 words. Now go listen to their records. Watch videos of them. Find specific instances of their playing that encapsulate the reasons why you love them. Put the songs or videos in a playlist and soak them up. See if you can mimic any aspect of what you hear without transcribing the exact notes. Record yourself doing this and listen back. Can you hear the essence of that guitarist in what you're playing? If not, try to determine what's missing. Then repeat this exercise.

THIS YEAR Do the above with 12 different musicians, one per month. Choose a variety of players.

CHAPTER 5:

MAKE TIME FOR SERIOUS PLAY

TIP: Be Your Own Jam Buddy

Recording yourself, playing along, and listening back is one of the most illuminating practice techniques available to us in the 21st century.

▶ To jam with yourself, you'll need:

- Your guitar
- A metronome
- Some kind of recording device

Take a short, simple chord progression. Eight bars is long enough. With the metronome ticking away and your recording device on, play one chorus of rhythm that feels easy and natural to you. When you come to the end of the eighth bar, improvise a solo and keep the chords going in your head. When you come up to the eighth bar of your solo, switch back to the rhythm.

As you listen back, play along, and reverse the roles. When you play rhythm on tape, play a solo in real life (and vice versa).

▶ Three reasons to jam with yourself:

1. It's a chance to work on your rhythm. Any chance to work on rhythm guitar is good.

2. It works your soloing skills in a particular way. Play a short solo within a specific structure that feels like a complete statement with a beginning, middle, and end.

3. Listening. A lot of us don't take the time to listen to ourselves. We may practice and practice with a metronome or by ourselves, but that generally doesn't give us an opportunity to hear how we sound as a rhythm player or reacting to another musician.

THINGS TO DO

TODAY Jam with yourself. 10–15 minutes is all you need.

THIS MONTH Do it regularly. Stick with the same framework (key/chord progression/groove/tempo) for a few days, or until you get bored. Before you move on to a new framework, listen back to how you sounded on day one versus day three. Ask yourself, what changed? What stayed the same?

THIS YEAR Make a list of the keys, chord progressions, grooves, and tempos you want to feel more comfortable playing in. When you feel compelled to return to this exercise, mix and match the possibilities to create a framework to practice that both excites you and challenges you.

TIP: Put That Capo to Work

Many guitar players look at the capo as a crutch or a cheat. It's neither!

Capos are so useful in recording sessions, on gigs, and when writing music. They open up the possibilities of the guitar and can open up your imagination. *How?* Difference in range makes for a difference in sound. Think of a violin versus a viola, or alto versus tenor sax. Even when they're playing the same notes, they sound quite different. Capo-ing does the same to a guitar.

▶ The capo creates a new instrument

Raising your guitar's pitch with the capo can make it sound and feel like another instrument, perhaps reminiscent of a mandolin or ukulele or a different sort of guitar. The change of scene can recalibrate your creativity and refresh the ears of your listeners.

ADAM: *In the early 1990s, when I lived in San Francisco, I used to go see a guitar player named Jeff Linsky. He regularly played solo-guitar gigs on a requinto (a nylon-string guitar tuned a perfect 4th higher than standard tuning). His beautiful arrangements sounded like nothing I'd ever heard before—in part because of his fresh musical approach, and in part because he was in an uncommon register.*

▶ Open strings, everywhere

Another way the capo opens things up is that it gives you access to open-string vocabulary that's idiomatic to the guitar in any key, in that same higher range.

Things become possible that wouldn't quite be possible any other way. Well, people will pull off some incredible finger gymnastics to make it happen—but it doesn't ring and chime the same way unless you have the open strings working with you.

▶ Sitting in the mix

In a recording session, using a capo can help you focus on frequencies you want to bring out. If there's a complicated arrangement with many instruments and a lot going on, you'll want to narrow the range of what you're playing so that when you listen back, your part doesn't get lost in the mix.

Instead of turning the track louder, play your part higher. This can also be true when you're playing live: instead of asking the monitor engineer if you can get more guitar, rethink what you're playing, and see if you can get out of the way of whatever else is happening on stage. In other words, EQ yourself!

Intonation can get wonky as you move a capo up the neck, so you'll need to retune for each new capo position. There's a great series of videos online of James Taylor teaching how to play his songs, and at one point he brings up a trick for tuning with a capo. He'll tune certain strings slightly flat, which compensates for the change in intonation.

THINGS TO DO

TODAY Order a capo if you don't have one. If you do have one, put it on your guitar—any position that doesn't scrunch your fingers too much will do. Strum open major, minor, and dominant 7th chords, listening for the pitch of the new transposed chord that the familiar shape gives you. (If you're capo'd on the 3rd fret, for example, an open G major shape now gives you a B♭ chord!)

THIS MONTH Play songs you know with the capo on. Play songs you previously played with barre chords in open position. Transpose other songs to new keys.

THIS YEAR As you get more comfortable using the capo in different musical contexts at home, bring it to gigs and sessions. Look for contexts to use the capo that other musicians may not expect but that sound good to you.

TIP: Write Yourself Some Tunes

When it comes to composition, what we have found most helpful is to work within some predefined parameters. To be confronted with a blank slate can cause a bit of panic, and on the flip side, to start out being hyper-detailed about what you want to do can also get overwhelming. So, split the difference: give yourself just *a few* boundaries that you can work within.

▶ Here's a sample set to compose from:

- Length: 16 bars
- Key: G♯ minor
- Mood: Bluesy
- Bonus: Start on a chord that isn't the tonic

▶ Other parameters you can draw on:

- Tempo
- Form
- Arc
- Don't do something that you tend to do often

Then, improvise a melody within the boundaries you've set. Record it into a looper pedal or your DAW (digital audio work-station) of choice so you can be sure of what you played.

Listen back to it and start to think about harmonic choices that you'd like to make. If you're not sure what to do or are having trouble hearing anything, add a bass line to it first. That will narrow down your options for harmony/chord qualities. Then, make incremental adjustments—harmonic, melodic, or even in form—until you're satisfied.

You don't need to throw the whole kitchen sink into a piece of music or be too precious about it. The sheer act of writing music is the point. Whether or not it's something you want to play again doesn't necessarily matter. If you write a lot of music often, you'll invariably find things you'll keep.

THINGS TO DO

TODAY Challenge yourself to start a piece of music and finish it in one session.

THIS WEEK Write a new piece of music every night before you go to bed. Set a timer for 30 minutes and check in with it periodically throughout your writing session.

THIS YEAR In January and July, write a song a day for a month, and upload it to songadayforamonth.com.

PART II: CHALLENGES

The material in this section is designed to be worked with over a longer period of time. Even though we'll still list things you can do today, there's no need to hurry through anything in these chapters or expect anything to be fully integrated into your playing after one practice session. This section may also require a little more effort on your end for it to bear fruit. However, that means the musical growth that results will be unique to you. Work hard, and have fun!

CHAPTER 6:
BUILD DEEPER CONNECTIONS

CHALLENGE: Sound Good by Yourself

If you've never played solo guitar before, it can feel daunting, like jumping into the deep end of a pool before you've learned to swim. Even if you have played some solo guitar gigs, it might still feel that way. Whatever your level of experience, playing guitar alone will always be an opportunity to learn and grow.

ADAM: *In the mid-'90s, I decided I wanted to learn to play solo guitar. I was a big fan of Tuck Andress (the guitarist from Tuck & Patti), Joe Pass, and Ted Greene (who I got to study with a little bit). These guys could make the guitar sound like a piano—or even like a small orchestra. I was really intrigued by that and wanted to carve out some space to explore the idea further. So I went to the local café in my neighborhood and asked if I could play there every Sunday.*

They didn't have much money to pay me, but it wasn't about the money. It was an opportunity to play solo guitar for three hours, on a weekly basis, in front of real people. It was a low-pressure situation because people were generally more interested in their eggs and bacon than they were in my music.

One of the many things I got out of the experience was the importance of sounding good by yourself. For me, it wasn't about learning more chord voicings or fancy turnarounds. It was actually about learning to play more minimally. I learned that instead of playing, say, a Dmaj7 chord on five strings at once, I could just play the bass note and the melody note, with maybe one harmony note in between, every so often. This started to sound as rich to me as chords with more notes—and it was a lot easier to grab.

Here's some irony: Ted Greene was a master of solo guitar and knew more chords than anybody I've ever seen, yet he told me in one of our lessons together that he didn't think I should spend my time working out fancy solo guitar arrangements. It can be a recipe for disaster, he said. You work up these really complicated arrangements, creating so many chances to trip yourself up, and then get frustrated because you didn't play things exactly right. Where's the fun in that?

Instead, Greene encouraged me to play melodies—beautifully and clearly—with simple chord voicings and infectious rhythms. So that's what I did, and you can do your own version of that too. Whatever music is interesting to you, see if you can approach it on the guitar in a way that's simple and straightforward. That doesn't mean dumbing it down, it means eliminating all the stuff that's unnecessary so that the melody and groove are clear.

THINGS TO DO

TODAY Is there a song stuck in your head today? Learn to play the melody on the guitar, sweetly, clearly, and powerfully. Solo guitar has often been referred to as *chord-melody* style, but it's really the other way around. Try to think of it as *melody-chord*. The melody comes first.

THIS MONTH Make a list of five songs you like to play. Learn to play them with just the bass notes and melodies, together.

THIS YEAR Get a weekly gig—brunch or otherwise. Record yourself weekly, and listen back to track your progress.

CHALLENGE: Consider the Emotional Contour

When we learn to improvise, the first thing that we're often confronted with is *chord-scale theory*. First you learn scales, and then, you learn how those scales relate to particular chords. Of course, this is good information to know, but it doesn't tell you how to shape your solo. When we think of great solos, the ones we remember have a distinct shape to them.

Working with the idea of *emotional contour* can help you create a narrative to your improvising and keep it from sounding like an unrelated series of notes and scale patterns. This is something you can control and be intentional about; it doesn't have to be something that you notice after the fact when you listen back to a recording of your playing.

When it's your turn to play a solo, instead of thinking "I'm going to fill that space with E minor pentatonic scales," think about it in terms of the emotional contour that you want to build. That doesn't necessarily mean you won't be playing E minor pentatonic ideas, but thinking about it in terms of how you play (instead of what you play) will imbue your music with a sense of personality that no one but you can convey.

▶ How to raise the stakes in a solo:

- Play higher
- Play faster
- Play louder

- Harmonic tension: go outside the chord or tonal center, or play free
- Harmonic density: play more than one note at a time
- Surprise: play something nobody was expecting (perhaps not even you!)
- A quick change: instead of easing into something, take a left turn and go there immediately
- Special effects: harmonics, going slightly out of tune, open strings, any combination of those
- Extended techniques

▶ Raising the stakes in the opposite direction:

- Play lower
- Play slower
- Play quieter
- Harmonic clarity: state the obvious
- Play a quote or cliché: something obvious

Lots of music has emotional contour built into it already. For example, if you play a song like "Stella By Starlight," two-thirds of the way through there's a natural peak that's achieved by both melodic and harmonic movement: the melody is hitting its highest notes, and the harmony is far off from where the song started.

However, if you're playing music that's more static harmonically (i.e., over one or two chords), you have a lot of freedom to build whatever shape you want.

THINGS TO DO

TODAY Make a backing track for yourself or play along to an existing one. Get out a pencil and a piece of paper and draw some doodles. Decide how many measures that doodle represents, whether it's 4, 8, 16, or however many, and see if you can follow that line. Don't worry about "right" and "wrong" notes. Concentrate on energy. Rises and falls, peaks and valleys.

THIS WEEK Make an "emotional contour transcription" of three of your favorite solos. Take three solos you absolutely love (by guitarists or not), count out how many measures they are, and draw out the shape of the solo over a period of time. Once you've done that for three different solos, improvise your own solos using your doodles as a roadmap.

THIS MONTH Whenever you play with other people, challenge yourself to improvise an emotional contour every time you take a solo. See if you can follow the line you're tracing in your head with the music you're playing on your guitar.

CHALLENGE: Play Music in Every Key

There are twelve major keys and twelve minor keys. You should spend time practicing in all of them. This is a requirement for any player aiming to be a more complete guitarist/musician: not only being able to play songs in the typical guitar keys, but also being able to move a song to any key you want.

The way the guitar works, it's easy enough to scoot your hand from one position to another when wanting to play a chord grip or scale pattern somewhere else. However, transposition is about the *relationships* between notes and chords—being able to hear and play those relationships independent of the pitches themselves. So, playing music in motion is ultimately going to be more valuable than practicing isolated chords on different parts of the neck.

▶ Transposing chords

When you're moving a piece of music around to different keys, it helps to consider the notes and chords as numbers (be they roman numerals or "Nashville numbers") as opposed to their actual note names. For example, a I-V-vi-IV chord progression in D and B♭ may sound different and use different pitches, but the distance from one chord to the next is always the same: they're still I-V-vi-IV, no matter what key you're in.

▶ Transposition exercise:

1. Take two chords that belong in a given key: say, I and IV in the key of C. Play them in sequence, 12 times in a row, in a new key each time. Use the circle of 5ths/4ths, so you don't have to decide which key you're going to play next.
2. Add a third chord and do it again.
3. Do this with different groups of chords from a key (stick to the diatonic major chords). Over time, hit on all the different combinations of two or three chords (out of the seven chords in a diatonic major key). As you get comfortable moving around between two to three chords in multiple keys, hearing how they orbit whatever key you're in, you're getting closer to being able to transpose real music! So, let's try it...
4. Take a short, simple folk song (something with three or four chords, but a longer form than the above exercises) and go through it in 12 different keys, as you did in the first step.

▶ Transposing melodies

When you transpose any given melody or melodic phrase, you'll need to understand which scale degrees it's made up of (including non-diatonic notes, if there are any). Be sure to keep in mind what scale degree you begin and end on, and note the overall direction of the line.

If a song is longer than 16 measures or so, split the song up into digestible sections, and work on transposing one section at a time.

Many jazz standards have different sections in different keys. When you transpose songs like these, you're *really* getting a workout. For example, "The Song Is You" has an A section in C but moves up a minor 3rd to E major in the bridge. If you play that song in a few different keys, that leap won't feel like an anomaly after a while.

One big reason to practice songs in multiple keys is that every singer has a different vocal range. If you play songs with a singer, or you yourself are singing, chances are that you'll want to learn a song in a different key to accommodate the range of the singer. When it's just you, you can take your time working it out, but in a sideman situation, you may not know what key somebody's going to want to play in until the moment they tell you.

At a beginner or intermediate level, most people play tunes in the same keys, but as you start to play with more seasoned players, you'll notice they are playing in a lot of different keys—either for the challenge or because a particular key makes the range of their instrument speak. You can make that choice too. As you take a song through multiple keys, you'll find it probably lays on the fretboard in certain keys better than others.

On the gig, or even in the rehearsal, isn't the ideal moment to realize, *"Oh, I should practice in this key more."* Practice it more *now*. Then, if it comes up in real life on a gig, you'll be glad you did the work.

THINGS TO DO

TODAY Take a song you know well and write a chord chart of it in the original key. Then write three more charts for this song, in three other keys.

THIS MONTH Practice, and memorize, all four charts you've made.

THIS YEAR Thoroughly memorize a dozen songs you're already familiar with, each in the original key. Once memorized, regularly practice (and perform, if possible) this repertoire in every key *but* the standard keys.

CHAPTER 7:
TUNE IT UP

CHALLENGE: Bend in Tune

Bending in tune is a skill that can make the difference between a good guitar player and a great guitar player. As soon as a guitar player starts bending, you can hear whether that's something they've spent time on and care about, or not.

Bending out of tune is an easy habit to get into, chiefly because a lot of us practice without any external pitch reference. If you're sitting in your practice room bending away unaccompanied, you don't necessarily hear that the note that you arrived on at the top of your bend is flat or sharp.

To bend in tune doesn't always mean that your note would land right up the middle if you were looking at a tuner. You can be expressive and be slightly flat or sharp: it's not about being right on the dot. What it *is* about is being in control and not having intonation be an afterthought.

It's important to hear your bending as bending *into* a note rather than hitting a note and bending away from it. Your fingers know where you're starting, but somebody listening is going to focus on where you arrived much more than where you begin. Think about where you're going as much as, or even more than, where you're coming from. The starting note may not even register to the listener. Think about your favorite string benders: when they bend a note, you don't think, "Oh man, they slid away at the perfect time." You think, "Wow, they really stuck the landing!" The same is true for whoever listens to you.

ADAM: *A note about the mechanics of bending: Generally, I'm thinking about pushing into the fretboard, and then up. You can't actually press into the fretboard, but it's a feeling that helps create more strength. If you're just moving up and down, your fingers may not have enough leverage to keep the string where you want it.*

▶ To practice bending in tune, it helps to use both a pitch and time reference

Pitch

Play against a drone note that's limited to roots and 5ths. You could do this with a looping pedal, but if you don't have one, check out the iSruthi app.

A shruti box is something that's often used in Indian music. Even if you don't know anything about Indian music, you've probably heard it—the drone of roots and 5ths. Bending notes in the key that's droning provides a constant pitch reference to hear your bending against and moderate your touch to.

Drones are better than backing tracks. You want something pure and simple that doesn't pull toward major or minor.

Time

In general, practicing in time as much as possible is encouraged, and that applies to bends as well. You can have a metronome ticking away quarter notes, or a drum loop that you like.

We also recommend the TimeGuru app—it has a *random mute* function that takes away clicks at whatever percentage you set it to. This can further hold you accountable to developing a stronger internal clock.

If the drone plus metronome combination bugs your ears, use a looping pedal to record yourself playing something in rhythm. Get your own groove going to play on top of.

▶ Other tips for bending practice:

- Warm up for 10–15 minutes before you start doing these exercises.
- If you're playing plugged in, turn your reverb off. It makes it easier to hear the accuracy of your tuning (or lack thereof).
- As you bend, avoid vibrato for now. It keeps your ear from hearing whether you bent in tune.
- In the moment, your intonation may not always be clear, so record yourself and listen back. Upon listening, decide what's working and what might need more practice.
- If you find yourself over or under-shooting, spend extra time on that note. Figure out what you're doing that's making it sound that way.
- Make sure you practice bends with each of your left-hand fingers. Over time, you should be able to bend at least a full step with any finger (on an electric guitar). If you use the higher fingers (ring or pinky) you can always support them with your other fingers. This is how most people do it.
- If you're new to bending, practice it on lighter strings, on an electric guitar. As your fingers gain strength, and if you prefer, you can move up to a heavier gauge/tension incrementally.
- If you're spending more than one day in a row working on bending, try to use the same guitar for consistency.

ETHAN: *I find that my bends become more consistently in tune if my hands are calibrated to the strings and scale length of one instrument, rather than having to constantly adjust between the peculiarities of multiple guitars.*

▸ Step-by-step routine to dial in your bends using a drone (and optional metronome):

STEP 1: Bend into the note that's droning. Start from a half step away, then a whole step away, then a minor 3rd (if you can swing it).

STEP 2: Keeping the drone going, bend into major and minor pentatonic scales all over the fretboard. All the bends that exist within those pentatonic scales are made up of whole steps and minor 3rd—lots of opportunity to get your wider-interval bends clear. Move around between different positions. Depending on what you're comfortable with, you could organize this by the five pentatonic boxes or move up and down the neck, not limiting yourself to a box. The big idea is to cover as much of the fretboard as you can, in whichever way makes the most sense to you.

STEP 3: Play the seven major scale modes against your drone note (i.e., if you're playing a D drone note, play D major, D Dorian, D Phrygian, etc.). Bend from one scale note to another.

STEP 4: If you want to go farther with scales, whatever note you're droning could be any of the seven notes in a melodic minor scale or harmonic minor scale. Truth be told, there are so many scales (whole tone, diminished, scales you invent, etc.), and the drone note could be part of any of them. Whatever scalar/harmonic vocabulary you're working into your playing, bend into it.

STEP 5: Once you get the hang of this, start to play real melodies. Play easy songs that everybody knows (i.e., "Amazing Grace," "Shenandoah," even "Happy Birthday"). Play songs you like. If you're an improviser, improvise some new melodies!

▶ More bending activities:

- *Unison bending* is when you bend one string to sound the same note as a string that's not bent. As you try it, you'll first hear a pulsing sound—commonly known as *beating*—which tells you that the two notes aren't quite in tune with each other. When the beating dissolves, they are.
- *Pre-bending* is when you bend up to a note, but don't pick it until you're already bent. When you pick the note and release the bend, it sounds like you bent backward!
- *Double-stop bends* are another frontier worth exploring. You bend two strings with two fingers in the same fret. Depending on your level of control and which strings you're bending, you can eventually bend each string a different distance—say, up a half step on the 2nd string and up a whole step on the 3rd string. It doesn't have to be that dialed in to sound good though. Hitting the "in-between" notes is a sound unto itself. These are a lot easier if you're using a plain, unwound 3rd string. If your 3rd string is wound, it tends to take a lot more work to bend it where you want it.

Bending in tune is something we can all work on, no matter what level we're at. It's a skill you can liken to a muscle—if you don't exercise it regularly, it tends to atrophy. So, if you like to bend, bend in tune!

CHALLENGE: Get Comfortable in Alternate Tunings

Alternate tunings can intimidate a lot of players. If you're an experienced guitarist already (perhaps even out gigging and recording), the thought of purposefully taking your guitar out of standard tuning, a place you know so well, and into unfamiliar territory can be scary!

Why would you want to do that? Well, tunings beyond the standard EADGBE are a Pandora's box of new sounds. You have access to sounds that you can't get in standard tuning—certain kinds of chord voicings and drones. It's like an expanded register of sounds all available in easy, non-stretchy grips.

If you feel scared of the unknown fretboard, turn that idea around. Treat the guitar as a brand-new instrument. Remember how excited you were when you first picked up the guitar and really didn't know anything, but that's what made it fun? That's a place that alternate tunings can become for you.

▸ A five-step process you can use to get to know any tuning new to you

We will use double drop D as an example. To get to double drop D, first tune the low E down a whole step to D. Then tune the high E down a whole step to D. Now, we have DADGBD.

There are a lot of cool things about this tuning, most especially that it sounds a like it's in two keys at once. You have DAD on the bottom three strings: root/5th/root in the key of D. The upper three strings are a G major triad, GBD. So, it's a great tuning for songs in either key, or songs that switch between two keys a 4th or 5th apart.

 ADAM: *I love double drop D tuning. When I think of playing in non-standard tunings, it's the first one I usually go to. I've written songs in this tuning, and I've also used it in the studio to come up with different kinds of sounds when I'm overdubbing guitars on other people's records.*

1. Find what's familiar

Most every tuning will have something you've seen before. What can you go back to if you feel totally lost and need to find something comfortable? In the case of our example tuning, the middle four strings are unchanged.

In the realm of open-position chords alone, that means you can play C major, A minor, or A major—and play those shapes farther up the neck, too. In fact, you can play a 4-string chunk of any chord shape you know, provided it's in the zone of familiarity. If you're playing melodic ideas, you can keep them on those strings.

2. Find what's new, and combine with the old

In this tuning, the new would be the octave Ds on either side. There are a lot of sounds to be found by playing the chord shapes you already know and adding one or both of the outside strings to them. A simple C major becomes a Cadd9, and an Am becomes an Am11! There's a lot of discovery to be had by thinking about what chords might sound cool with the D note droning on top or bottom.

3. **Learn a cover song native to this tuning**
   Learn something that was written in this tuning. The shapes will fall easily under your fingers, even if they're slightly unfamiliar. Playing in a new tuning doesn't have to mean endlessly floundering around, looking for stuff. Take advantage of songs that already exist, and build confidence by seeing that you can make music in this tuning.

   A few songs in double drop D:
   - "Cinnamon Girl," Neil Young
   - "The Chain," Fleetwood Mac
   - "Going to California," Led Zeppelin
   - "Don't Let It Bring You Down," Neil Young (same tuning intervals, lowered a whole step)

   If you happen to come across another tuning, or invent your own, try a web search to see if you can find songs that already exist in that tuning. The music of Joni Mitchell is an excellent resource for less common alternate tunings, and her website (jonimitchell.com) has a complete database of all the tunings for every song she's ever recorded.

4. **Learn to play a song that's not native to this tuning**
   Take either a cover song or one of your own songs and try to make it work in this tuning. If you want things to sound the same, you'll have to finger differently. On the flip side, fingering something the same way will give you new sounds. Both are cool—use your taste and musicality to make choices about what you like and want to keep as you create this new arrangement.

5. Write a song

If you're not a songwriter, write a song anyway. Use a clear form: it can be just a verse and a chorus, or an A and B section of an instrumental tune. If you are a songwriter, write a whole song. Creating something from scratch engages a different part of your brain than learning other people's songs, and it's essential for your musical growth.

CHAPTER 8:

PLAY NICELY WITH OTHERS

CHALLENGE: Play Nicely with Vocalists (Hint: It's Not About You)

This section is geared toward those of you who play guitar to accompany a singer. If it's not about you, what else could it be about? The big picture, of course! In the big picture, the singer is the main event. What can you play so that everything the singer sings sounds great?

▶ Some ways a guitar player can get in the way of a vocalist:

- Playing too loud
- Playing too much
- Playing in the singer's range
- Playing in the singer's rhythm

▶ Things you can do to accompany and complement a vocalist:

- Find a good balance of volume between the guitar and voice.
- Develop a sense of what your singer's register is in the song you're playing and fill around it by playing lower or higher.
- Listen for the rhythm of the vocal line. If it's a percussive melody, with a lot of eighth and sixteenth notes, try playing longer tones—dotted quarters or half notes. If they're starting

phrases on downbeats, start your phrases on upbeats, and play things that cross over bar lines.

- Listen to the timbre of their voice. Make choices about your equipment that don't muddy up the sound when you play together.

▸ Things to consider if the singer plays guitar, too

If they're strumming chords, play something smaller, like two-note or three-note chords. If they're playing open chords on the lower end of the neck, put a capo on and get out of their register!

This approach has you thinking more like an orchestrator: an orchestra doesn't play all the same notes in the same register. There are some people playing the bass frequencies, some on the midrange, and others in the upper registers. All of the harmonies work together nicely—no mud—and all of the melodies are clear because they're not stepping on each other.

It's about the singer, it's about the song, and it's about you doing anything you can to help the singer sound as good as they can. Think about where you can fit in and be a benefit, asset, and value to the music.

THINGS TO DO

TODAY Work on a simplified guitar accompaniment part for one song you might play with a singer. If it's a jazz-oriented song, use shell-style, three-note voicings, or even rootless voicings, to keep the harmony uncluttered. If it's in another style where shell chords aren't appropriate, use simple chord shapes (perhaps with a capo) and a clearly defined picking or strumming pattern.

THIS MONTH Make a list of five songs you like to play. Apply the same approaches as listed above.

THIS YEAR Cultivate a working partnership with a singer. Work through their repertoire, refining your approach to each song. Play some gigs together. Make a record together. Also, throughout the year, seek out and listen to recordings where guitarists are tastefully crafting accompaniment parts behind singers.

CHALLENGE: Play Nicely with Pianists

Note: This section is oriented mainly toward a jazz context.

The pairing of guitar and piano is often talked about among jazz musicians as particularly difficult to play well in. However, great piano/guitar duet albums abound that prove this isn't necessarily true. Two fantastic examples are Bill Evans and Jim Hall (*Undercurrent, Intermodulation*) and Fred Hersch (*Songs We Know* with Bill Frisell, *Free Flying* with Julian Lage).

▶ Four tips to keep in mind when playing in a duo:

1. **Keep your chords vague, yet straightforward**
   If you're playing alone, you may voice all notes in a four-note chord. When playing with a pianist, however, you might like to just play the upper part of the chord (without the root note), or a quartal voicing (interval of a 4th, slightly more spread out between the voices). In a duo, it's best not to use too many altered chords—that's the stuff that can get a little thorny.

2. **Rhythm is king**
   When people talk about the difficulty of guitar and piano together, they're usually talking about the notes. They will actually often work themselves out as long as you're simpatico rhythmically. So, get your own time in order, and try to find a pianist that feels time similarly to you, or one whose time you'd like to get closer to.

3. Listen ahead

Music moves forward. Start to develop a sensibility of not only where a pianist is in *this* moment, but where they might be going in the next moment. Try to listen to where they're going and what their tendencies are.

4. Sound

You can adjust the tone of your instrument much more easily than a pianist can theirs (on an acoustic piano, at least). Try to dial in your sound so that it nests nicely with the piano and doesn't muddy up the low end.

ADAM: *I used to play a lot with a drummer named Brannen Temple. I was always amazed that when I'd be going for these things in my solos, his drum fills would always catch what I was doing. He had a good intuition for listening, not just to what I was doing in a particular moment, but to where I seemed to be going.*

ETHAN: *Don't be afraid to ask your piano-playing buddy to leave some space for you to play, or let them know that you want to create something together. If you show you're there to listen, chances are they'll want to do the same for you.*

THINGS TO DO

TODAY Play along with a solo piano recording. Here is a handful to get you started:

• *Thelonious Alone in San Francisco,* Thelonious Monk

- *Live at Maybeck Recital Hall, Vol. 16*, Hank Jones
- *Vignettes,* Marilyn Crispell
- *Alone*, Bill Evans
- *Soliloquy,* Alan Pasqua
- *Solipsism,* Joep Beving
- *Solo Piano*, Chilly Gonzales
- *A Thousand Days*, Mitchell Froom

THIS MONTH Get together with a pianist to play in a duo.

THIS YEAR Get a regular duo gig with a pianist. Develop a repertoire. Make a record!

CHALLENGE: Play Nicely in a Trio

We are speaking specifically about a jazz trio here (with guitar, bass, and drums). Your repertoire may be songs from the jazz canon, or you may be playing original music that you describe as "jazz." Ideally, there'll be improvisation and interplay between the three musicians. That's not to say what's discussed here can't be applied to other types of music, but for the sake of simplicity, we'll limit ourselves to a jazz lens.

▶ Play in a trio

Get together with some friends, book a gig, rehearsal, or jam, and actually do it. You will learn so much by trying it and seeing what happens. Record your gig/rehearsal/jam, and let it sit for maybe 5–10 days. Then, go back and listen to it. Get out your notebook and take some notes. What's working? What's not working?

You'll gain so much insight specific to *you* by listening to yourself and your bandmates and giving yourself some honest feedback. You can also share the recording with a teacher, a trusted friend, or the people you played with in the first place.

▶ Listen to other trios

There are many great guitar trio records, in many different flavors. People have been doing this for a long time, and you don't have to reinvent the wheel. In fact, it's good to check out well-established wheels. You can also listen to other kinds of trios—piano and sax trios for example. There are so many great jazz and jazz-adjacent records where there are just three people playing.

▸ Work on your sound

If you're going to be the lead voice in your trio, then your sound should be deserving of other people's attention. If your sound isn't happening, then your trio isn't going to be happening. It's hard for us to say exactly what would improve *your* sound but refer back to "Play in a Trio" above—record yourself, listen back, make notes, and evaluate.

▸ Don't fear the open spaces

One approach to playing in a trio is to fill up as much space as you possibly can. It's surely one way to play, but it has to be done immaculately to not sound hurried and anxious. It can also be taxing on people's ears and imagination. Space is good—it helps draw people in.

▸ Practice rootless voicings

More often than not, the bass player is going to play the root, so you don't *need* to double it all the time. Try just playing the upper voices of a chord, or even a two-note version of it. This can give your trio a more open sound.

▸ Use open strings

Open strings are especially useful in a trio setting because they can fill up some harmonic space. They're available in lots of keys, and they don't have to necessarily be the root or 3rd. They could be an extension like the 9th.

▸ You don't have to play jazz standards

Even if you have a jazz trio, you could write music that both suits you and takes advantage of the format you're in. You could also arrange "non-jazz" songs and repurpose them for your group.

▸ Alternate roles

The guitar can go back and forth between playing melodic ideas and comping. It takes practice, so take a blues or standard song form, and start simple: solo for two bars, comp for two bars. You can accentuate this by playing the melodic parts a little louder, and the comping a little quieter.

When you're comfortable with that, you could try different variations of when you alternate roles. It doesn't have to be symmetrical. You could solo for one bar, comp for three. Once you get the hang of doing it through a more formulaic approach, you can free it up. Don't preplan the bars. Try to have a conversation with yourself and see how musical you can make it.

▶ Choose guitar-friendly keys

Make the most of the instrument you're playing, and put the melody in a register where it speaks on your guitar. There's no reason you have to play songs in the same key as *The Real Book*. This can also help you make the tune your own—it sets your arrangement/recording/performance apart from what people have done.

ADAM RECOMMENDS:

→ *The Jimmy Giuffre 3*, Jimmy Giuffre 3 (Jim Hall, guitar)
→ *A Night at the Vanguard*, Kenny Burrell
→ *Guitar Sounds from Lenny Breau*, Lenny Breau
→ *Intercontinental*, Joe Pass
→ *Live!* Jim Hall Trio
→ *Shinola*, John Scofield
→ *One Time Out*, Paul Motian Trio (Bill Frisell, guitar)
→ *Question and Answer*, Pat Metheny
→ *Right Brain Patrol (Ben Monder, guitar)*, Marc Johnson
→ *American Hips*, Jim Campilongo Trio
→ *Who Said Gay Paree?* Jakob Bro
→ *Arclight*, Julian Lage

ETHAN RECOMMENDS:

→ *The Poll Winners,* The Poll Winners (Barney Kessel, guitar)
→ *Closer,* Paul Bley (piano, instead of guitar)
→ *Bright Size Life,* Pat Metheny
→ *Two Drink Minimum,* Wayne Krantz
→ *Gone, Just Like a Train,* Bill Frisell
→ *Monk,* Peter Bernstein Trio
→ *Love Hurts,* Julian Lage
→ *Worry Later,* Adam Levy, Ben Goldberg, Smith Dobson

THINGS TO DO

TODAY Listen to some records from the recommendations given here.

THIS MONTH Arrange a tune for a trio (guitar, bass, drums). Choose a key that lets the song bloom on the guitar. Have a clear intro and ending. Include sections for improvisation. Write out your arrangement so that you can play it with bass and drums.

THIS YEAR Play as many trio gigs and informal jam sessions as you can. Work up a repertoire—originals, standards, whatever you like. Record and release a trio album.

CHAPTER 9:

SING YOUR SONG

CHALLENGE: Memorize Tunes

Memorizing songs is something that you need to be able to do if you're going to play professionally. In the world of professional guitar playing, the songs we tend to memorize fall into two categories:

1. **"Jazz" tunes**
   This doesn't necessarily mean tunes that are in the jazz idiom so much as songs that people tend to interpret differently each time they're played—different in key, feel, tempo, arrangement, and harmonization.

2. **"Pop" tunes**
   Again, we're not talking about the pop genre per se, but rather a tune that people play the same way every time, usually following the original recorded arrangement, in the original key.

Take a jazz song like "I Love Paris." You could search for and find 20 or 30 completely different versions of that tune. If you were to call it at a jam session, rehearsal, or gig, you'd be more likely to make decisions on the fly with your fellow musicians on how you'd all like to play the tune. Whereas something like a Beatles song—say, "Eight Days a Week"—would more likely be played in a way that references the original arrangement and production.

Each approach requires a slightly different process and different challenges for your memory, ears, and hands. We don't claim to have "the ultimate secret," but here are some ideas that work for us:

▶ Rinse and repeat

If you're just beginning to learn a song, listen to it as much as possible. If it's a jazz song with lots of different recorded versions, make yourself a playlist of all those different versions and listen to them (Spotify and other streaming services have made this so easy). Try and get to know the song as raw material—and that's it. This is characteristic of the "jazz" realm. Once you know the tune, you'll play it a little differently every time, too.

If it's more of a "pop" song, it's likely that you'll have to memorize a specific guitar part, and there's probably one well-known recording that you'll need to learn from. Listen to it over and over and over and over. Put it on repeat, listen to it when you're in the shower, listen to it when you're driving, listen to it while you're sleeping—listen until you can't take it anymore!

It has to move from the place in your brain where you store new things that you're hearing for the first time to the same space as your favorite song of all time. If you can't get it to migrate from "new song" file to "favorite song" file, you're not going to be able to memorize it, so repetition is key!

▶ Focus on the foreground

What's the most important part of the tune? Whatever it is for you, learn that first. If it has lyrics, focus on the lyrics and try to memorize them, regardless of whether or not you plan to sing them.

If it's a pop tune that you're playing with a full band, there may be one specific part you need to play in each section of the song—that's your foreground. If it's a song in the jazz realm, prioritize the melody and the root motion. Not *necessarily* the specific thing the bass player on whatever recording played—just the bass notes of the chord progression. Are we going from 1 to 6 to 4 to 5, or from 1 to 5?

Don't worry about memorizing the chords as their absolute names—Am to C to D, for example. If you can hear the root motion and the melody, and how they move together, then the rest of the chords tend to reveal themselves fairly easily.

▶ Melody, melody, melody

Melodies are things you can sing, so sing them as much as you can. Treat every element of the song as its own melody. The main melody of a song is one melody, and the bass line is a melody, too. For a pop tune, any important instrumental part in the recording is its own melody. Chords and chord progressions repeat themselves across all different kinds of music. At the end of the day, a melody defines a song more than its chord progression.

▶ Play it everywhere

Pick up your guitar and play a melody that you know super well. Doesn't matter where it's from—dealer's choice! Then try playing it in another key. Then play it in a different octave.

You can get even more methodical with this if you like. Remember Wayne Krantz's "4-fret" idea we mentioned earlier in "Position Yourself"? See if you can play the melody in all four fret positions. Then, try playing it on one string, six times: once for each string, but try keeping it in the same key. You'll find that some keys work better than others, depending on your melody!

If you can play a melody you know well, all over the guitar, then you'll have no problem doing it with a new song.

▶ Make memorizing songs a priority

Here's the thing about memorizing tunes: if you don't have to, you won't. That's what we've found, anyway. If we make charts and keep looking at them, it's nearly impossible to memorize the tunes. As soon as the charts are hidden, a different kind of memory kicks in.

If you've got a solo gig where you are playing a bunch of tunes, don't bring your songbook: show up empty-handed and see how much music you can make without charts. How many songs could you play if you had to play a solo gig right now? Take stock of the things you already know. There's probably more than you realize.

▶ Write it down, then throw it out

Transcribing is also a very helpful way to memorize tunes. If you're listening to something you need to learn, write out all the things that you need to know. You could start with the melody, then chords, plus any specific guitar parts or arrangement notes—all the nitty-gritty details that we tend to miss when listening casually. Whatever is helpful for you, write it down. Then ball it up and throw it away, or at least hide it. If you get stuck looking at the paper, you're never going to get off the page.

What's the point of writing it down if I can't look at it afterward? The act of writing it down helps your brain make more sense of it, build connections, and get inside the music in an organized way.

Record yourself playing the piece while you're reading the chart you made, then make that the last time you read the chart. After that, play along with the recording you just made. If you mess up, it's no big deal because you have your recorded self to fall back on.

▶ Use your eyes to internalize forms

It's good to be able to scan a chart quickly and then look away. That way you can use your eyes to follow the conductor or bandleader or connect with your fellow players. This takes practice, of course.

Try looking at a chart and see if you can visually grab the first four bars. Then, close your eyes and play. As you get into the third bar or so, open your eyes and grab the next four bars, then close your eyes or look away. Whatever you do, don't look at the page!

Pay close attention to phrase lengths. How many measures does a particular phrase last? It's often four, or eight, but can be shorter or longer. Count those measures as you play the phrase. You'll feel when you need to open your eyes to see what's coming next.

Great musicians can look at eight bars at a time—or sixteen bars, maybe even a whole page of music—and just grasp it. Then they're able to look away and make the music. It doesn't happen overnight. It takes practice, so practice it. While we may write it down because we have to, music is fundamentally a *listening* art.

 ADAM: *I've had a lot of recording experiences where I'm reading charts on the session. By the second or third take of the same song, I don't want to be looking at the charts anymore. I play differently when my eyes are fixated on the page.*

THINGS TO DO

TODAY Thoroughly memorize one tune.

THIS MONTH Thoroughly memorize five tunes.

THIS YEAR Thoroughly memorize 40 tunes: one a week, with an occasional week off.

CHALLENGE: Get to Know a Jazz Standard

Many people these days learn jazz-era standards from a "fake book" such as *The Real Book*. That's fine (and more on that later), but you may find when you learn songs from scratch that way, they don't stick with you like a song that you've heard over and over again.

To get inside a song originally composed in the '20s, '30s, or '40s, it helps to do two things, and the internet is an invaluable resource for both of them. First, find the earliest published sheet music (Scribd.com is a good resource for this). Then, listen to several recordings in a range of styles, from various eras, and with different instruments and singers playing the melody. Hearing the ways other artists have interpreted a tune can help you settle into an interpretation of your own. Make a playlist on your favorite streaming service. Start with a version from the period the tune was written in, then one from a few years later, then even later, and then a modern take. Hearing what other people have done with the tune will give you a more complete picture of what it has to offer.

This was an approach that jazz musicians used and continue to use, even to internalize contemporary songs. Jazz lore has it that Ron Carter went to see *The Sandpiper* in a theater with score paper in hand so he could chart out "The Shadow of Your Smile" (the movie's theme song) before a Wes Montgomery session where he would record the song later that day.

There are at least three essential musical elements to keep in mind when getting to know a jazz standard: melody, rhythm, and harmony. Music is made up of other factors as well, but these are the fundamental building blocks that you'll internalize when learning any standard.

You'll find room for personal expression within all these elements. When listening to recordings on a streaming playlist and referencing the original sheet music, you can compare and contrast different musicians' approaches, in order to create an interpretation that feels good for you.

▶ Melody

The biggest difference between what you'll see on paper and what you hear on records is *phrasing*. You'll never hear a singer or instrumentalist phrase a melody as grid-like as you'd see it on a lead sheet. Listen to your playlist and notice the way each phrase pushes and pulls against the beat.

▶ Harmony

When you cross-reference original (or as old as possible) sheet music with recorded interpretations, you'll see and hear what various musicians added or subtracted relating to the harmony of a tune. We'll use "I Concentrate on You" by Cole Porter as an example. Here's the first phrase:

Figure 4. Excerpt from "I Concentrate on You" by Cole Porter.

The chord changes in the second bar are extrapolations of the melody note—you're still essentially playing an E♭ chord here, but the D gives you a major 7th, and the C gives you a major 6th.

In bar 3, there's a B♭+ triad, but the bass note is still E♭. That's essentially an E♭m Maj7 chord. In our experience, that's not how most people tend to play that bar—it's usually played as a B♭7♯5 (so that it functions as a V chord) or an A♭7♭5 (IV7). With the E♭ on the bottom, it's a *very* different sound. Sometimes interesting details like this get lost over the years. Play through different options and see which one sits best with you.

This is just the first four bars. It's a 32-bar tune and there are plenty more twists and turns along the way, each presenting a decision to be made as to whether you'll play it with the original harmony, or more like Ella Fitzgerald, Grant Green, Antonio Carlos Jobim, or Brad Mehldau (all of whom also recorded "I Concentrate on You").

When putting together harmonies that you like, keep in mind:

• How is what you're playing supporting the melody?

- How is what you're playing keeping things moving forward?
- Is what you're playing going to lead you to where you want to be four or eight bars from now?

▸ Rhythm

If you look at original sheet music for "I Concentrate on you," or listen to an original recording (likely a Broadway cast recording), you'll hear the rhythm that the composer, Cole Porter, intended—but it's a rhythm very much of its time. A lot of developments have happened in rhythm since 1939, not only in American music, but all over the world.

Again, your playlist will be invaluable. Follow your taste. Think about why you like or don't like what you're hearing.

▸ Write it out

If you have your own unique spin on the harmony or rhythm that differs from how it's commonly played, make a chart so that other people know where you're going. This is all the more true if you have a specific arrangement you'd like to play, whether it's yours or someone else's.

With whatever song you're learning, sit with it and grow to love it as a song, not a box you're checking off on your to-do list.

▶ **To sum it up:**

- Learn the melody.
- Listen to as many classic recordings as you can find.
- Make some decisions about the harmony.
- Write a definitive chart that has the changes you like.
- Play it. Start with one key, and once you can get through it comfortably in one key, do it in another. Then another, then another, until it becomes something you can really play music with.

It's a lot of work on the front end as you get to know any tune, but the reward is that you can play the song expressively, creatively, and in a personal way.

CHALLENGE: Don't Trust The Real Book

If you play jazz, you'll recognize this:

Figure 5. The Real Book. *Hal Leonard Publishing Corporation, 2004.*

It's *The Real Book,* a book of tunes (usually one per page). A lot of these tunes are jazz standards: songs written in the '30s and '40s, often for Broadway musicals, by people like George Gershwin and Cole Porter. There are also plenty of later tunes associated with bebop and post-bop: music from the '40s through the '60s and beyond.

At some point in time, people realized that there was this whole knowledge base of tunes that people played at jam sessions or gigs, and it would be good to compile them in one book. That way, if you were going to get together with people who didn't know all the same tunes as you, at least you'd have a repertoire to work from.

Books like this have existed for many years in various forms— books of tunes that you could use to fake it through a gig, with just the melody and chords, simply charted. The earlier books were called *fakebooks*. The one that came along as jazz education blossomed (and the one most commonly seen nowadays) is cleverly called *The Real Book*.

Ironically, we'd say, don't trust it. There's a danger in taking it too literally. There are a lot of inaccuracies. For example, take Thelonious Monk's "'Round Midnight." The changes are mostly there, but they're not exactly what Monk played. Even Monk himself didn't play it the same way every time.

The Real Book is a good place to start. If you were at a jam session or a gig, for instance, and somebody said, *"Let's play 'Round Midnight.' Here's the* Real Book *chart,"* that's fine. But if you *really* want to get inside a jazz tune, it's better to make your own charts.

 ADAM: *With all due respect to The Real Book, this is a common problem in music literature. When I was a teenager, I bought a songbook of Beatles songs. I was thrilled to own it. Music and lyrics for every song the Beatles ever recorded—yes! However, when I got home and started looking through the book with guitar in hand, I found that the notation didn't always match what I heard. Some songs were even written in different keys than the original recordings. The book didn't show how to play any of the specific guitar stuff, either.*

I learned a good lesson. Books are good for getting you part of the way there, but you always have to dig deeper on your own.

This parable goes beyond books. Don't trust the internet either. Although there's now an online lesson or user-generated tab available for virtually any song you'd ever want to learn on the guitar, it wasn't always that way.

If you're over 40, you might remember back when you had to figure stuff out for yourself or find somebody who knew the song and then pay or otherwise coax them to show it to you. That was the only way you could learn things—with your own ears, or by getting it from somebody who had figured it out. Now, you can simply search for a lesson on YouTube. That's fine, but it's not the same thing as figuring it out yourself. Put in the work and you'll be better for it.

THINGS TO DO

TODAY Take a familiar standard such as Cole Porter's "Night and Day," and learn it without *The Real Book*. Write out the melody as clearly and simply as you can. Add the chord changes, relying on your own sensibilities.

THIS MONTH Do the above exercise weekly, with classic tunes or other tunes you like to play.

THIS YEAR Assemble a book of your own. Use charts you've made yourself (or at least edited yourself) to reflect your musical taste.

CHAPTER 10:

PRACTICE WITH INTENTION

CHALLENGE: Don't Look Down!

We guitar players are always trying to shake a bad habit or two. If you know what yours are and want to rid yourself of them, it's not going to happen by sheer force of will. You have to practice playing the guitar without reverting to your bad habit—instead, playing with good habits! One of the most common bad habits we see is guitarists looking down at their hands.

▶ Here are three key reasons why it's better not to look down:

1. System overload

When you start looking at your hands while playing, your brain wants to make micro-corrections that slow down your activity. By the time your eyes are seeing, and your hands are reacting to your eyes, it's more likely that you're going to "spill something" as Adam would say.

ADAM: *Years ago, a friend of mine who worked as a waiter told me that if you're carrying a tray with cups of hot coffee, and you're worried about spilling it, the best thing you can do is not look at the tray. Look where you're going instead, and trust that your body can make the little adjustments to keep everything upright.*

"Wait," we can hear you saying. *"How am I going to know which fret or string I'm on if I'm not looking at it?!"* Music isn't a visual art. It's an aural and kinesthetic one. Think about all the amazing musicians in the world who've happened to be blind—Ray

Charles, Stevie Wonder, Raul Midón, and so on. Not having anything to look at sure didn't stop them, so why should it stop you?

2. Aches and pains

When you're turning your head to look at the fretboard, or down at your picking hand, you're straining muscles in the side and back of your neck. Doing that for 10, 20, 30 or more years can take a toll on your body.

 ETHAN: *This is a good spot to mention that not looking down doesn't mean keeping your head stiff and immobile, staring straight ahead. Overcorrection is my personal bad habit!*

3. Missed connections

When you keep your eyes open and above the guitar, you have the opportunity to look around at the people you're playing with. Maybe the bass player is trying to tell you something! If you're constantly glancing down at your guitar, it's like driving and only looking straight ahead, 10 feet in front of you. That's no way to drive! You need to look way ahead. You need to keep an eye on your peripherals. You need to check your rear-view mirror. Use your eyes to connect with your bandmates.

Of course, you can also use your eyes to connect with your audience, playing to somebody in the front row, back row, or anywhere in between. Personal connection is one of the real joys of playing music. As long as you're looking at your fretboard, you're not going to make much contact with anyone, onstage or off.

▶ Strategies

Not looking down when you're playing something relatively stationary (in one position on the fretboard) isn't all that difficult. However, shifting positions without looking is a little trickier. Here are some ideas to help strengthen that skill:

• Play scales and arpeggios, two notes per string.
• Play scales and arpeggios on a single string.
• Play the same note on every string.
• Play harmonized scales on multiple string sets.
• Play melodies to songs you know on a single string.
• Learn a classical piece that shifts positions throughout.
• Write an étude that shifts positions regularly.

Whatever *your* bad habit is, you'll need to figure out what you can practice that will challenge you to play with good habits instead.

THINGS TO DO

TODAY In your practice journal, make a list of your bad guitar habits.

THIS WEEK Focus on one bad habit. Create practice strategies to counteract it, and follow through with them.

THIS MONTH/YEAR Cycle around to a new habit from your list regularly. Periodically revisit the list, cross out habits that have improved, and add new ones that may have developed.

The point isn't to have zero bad habits on the list. We are all human, and by nature, imperfect. Growth is cyclical, not linear, and the more you can stay on top of habits as they crop up, the stronger your overall musicianship will be.

CHALLENGE: What Is Technique, Anyway?

Simply put, technique is the way you touch your instrument. We don't prescribe any one particular way to play. If you're attuned to the music you're making, you may find yourself using a variety of approaches within one song or even within a single phrase.

 ETHAN: *When I was in high school, I was chomping at the bit to make the guitar the focus of the rest of my life. I pushed myself too hard, played too much without stretching or warming up, always working at the upper limit of my abilities—and not in a good way.*

I ended up with tenosynovitis in both wrists. Thankfully, I never had to stop playing entirely, but I had to play a lot less. At a time when I wanted to be working the hardest and playing the most, I suddenly had to figure out how to hold onto the opportunity to play at all.

But the relief was only temporary. I spent an entire season seeing a hand therapist who specialized in repetitive stress injuries. She prescribed several arm, wrist, and hand stretches, deep-tissue massage, and icing. That all eased the pain I was feeling, but I still needed to figure out what I was doing wrong with the guitar to find myself in this predicament in the first place.

The thing that ultimately made a difference for me was the Alexander Technique. Essentially, the Alexander Technique (A.T.) is an approach to relearn how to move your body in the way that it's naturally designed, combating bad habits and unnecessary tension we've acquired without realizing it. I encourage you to read up on it and take a lesson yourself!

During the summer before I started college at the University of Southern California, I was taking weekly Alexander

Technique lessons with a teacher in my hometown, and I've studied intermittently elsewhere in the intervening years. I always learn new insights—and relearn old ones that I've since forgotten—about myself, my body, my mind, and how they all relate to the instrument.

Another thing that's helped me quite a lot is talking with peers, mentors, and heroes about how they do what they do. These conversations, along with experiences I've had myself, have led me to some thoughts about how we can have an easier time playing the guitar, physically speaking.

All of the following thoughts on technique are interconnected. Feel free to skip around and see how the ideas relate to one another.

▶ Learn to settle

ETHAN: *This is an idea that I got from hanging out with Bryan Sutton—one of my favorite guitarists who's a hero in both session musician and acoustic flatpicking worlds. When we first met and played together a few years ago, I was hell-bent on learning how to improvise on fiddle tunes with musicality and clarity at faster tempos.*

When I shared my difficulties in that area with Bryan, he told me that one roadblock he often sees in his students—regardless of their level—is an inability to physically settle. When working to increase our tempos, we can get so wound up that we play faster than we need to or mean to. That causes over-anticipation and anxiety, resulting in rushing and not playing things we'd like to hear. He encourages creating what he calls "habits of processing" while you play and listening to music that encourages your mind and body to settle. Here are a couple of those:

1. **If you feel tension somewhere in your body, leave it.**
   Don't react to it, judge it, or try to fix it. Instead, look for movements elsewhere in those moments. Can your eyes move? Can you swallow? Can you breathe? You always have three choices at the moment of noticing:

   • Keep doing what you've been doing
   • Don't do anything at all
   • Do something different.

   Play with all the options. What happens if you freak out? What happens if you analyze? What happens if you don't do anything at all? Know what these reactions feel like. Remind yourself that you're just playing music—it isn't life or death!

2. **Fast tempos don't require you to play a lot of notes to fill the space.**
   Instead of feeling each beat hyper-consciously, only register downbeats (1 and 3; just 1; or every other 1). Breathe along with those downbeats and play in a way that fits inside your breathing. Plenty of beautiful music can be made with half notes and whole notes.

▶ Play guitar with your whole body

Our fingers touch the strings to make the guitar sound, but the fact of the matter is that they're the end of the line. Beyond your fingertips, you've got knuckles, a palm, a wrist, a forearm, an elbow, an upper arm, a shoulder joint, a shoulder blade, a neck, a spine, and a head. Often, tension in our playing comes from one part of our body locking up or disengaging.

It's essential to appreciate that *everything* in your "physical supply chain" contributes to your approach to the instrument. That doesn't mean every part of your body is always doing something in a visible way. Ideally, each part feels light and available. You don't need to force this feeling. Remind yourself, each time you pick up your guitar: *that's* what you're going for.

▶ There's more time than it seems

The great classical guitarist, Scott Tennant, wrote a book called *Pumping Nylon*. Although Tennant's exercises and études are designed to bolster classical technique, all sorts of players can benefit from working on that material. One big thing that we got from it was an articulation of an idea that "retention of tension" is the culprit of many left-hand technical difficulties.

When we're playing new or unfamiliar material with the left hand, we tend to squeeze hard. So hard, in fact, that the "squeezed" feeling never quite leaves our hand after we've played, even when we are past the learning phase. That may manifest in the left hand holding onto notes long after they were intended to fade away. To get to the next note or chord, we then have to unstick the squeeze. That can feel like pulling apart two objects that have been glued together.

Carrying all that tension, from both the original squeeze and the unsticking, is a real drag. But there's hope! Because we've been inadvertently holding on longer than we need to, we can consciously release sooner than we previously thought—that gives us more time between chord changes and more time to let the tension dissipate from the left hand.

▶ Effortlessness comes from effortlessness

Your kinesthetic experience of playing something that feels very easy can be used as a reference point when learning new music. Think back to the first things you learned when you picked up the guitar. For many of us, that's the open-position chords: C major, G major, and so on. To play them now feels so familiar that there's not much conscious activity. You don't have to *try* to do anything, it just happens. Because of that, you can play these chords and observe other things about your playing, or pay attention to something else entirely. The execution of a familiar chord doesn't demand the entirety of your being at attention. That's a feeling. *Remember that feeling.*

 ETHAN: *A lot of my thinking about the relationship between technique and emotion is influenced by conversations I've had with the brilliant guitarist Julian Lage. These ideas about effortlessness, in particular, are cribbed straight from him (check is in the mail, Julian!).*

When you're learning a piece of music that requires more physical and mental bandwidth, alternate between playing something that's difficult and playing something that feels effortless. Returning to that easy feeling while learning something difficult is valuable because it can give you a better perspective on your own progress and it makes acquiring new skills feel a little less overwhelming.

▶ Visualize

Picture yourself playing guitar in your mind's eye. It probably looks and sounds exactly like it does when you're really playing, except it's all in your head—not your hands. The things that are challenging to play may remain that way. Here's the interesting thing, though: in your mind, you don't have to worry about *actually* moving your fingers, so you can play whatever you want. Chances are, when you pick up the guitar after visualizing yourself playing something difficult, you'll have a clearer idea of how to play it. Good practice is as much mental as it is physical.

This can also be a great way to keep improving if hand-fatigue is preventing you from playing your instrument as much as you'd like to. It may sound like woo-woo nonsense, but we've seen it work for us. Try it.

CHAPTER 11:

MAP THE FRETBOARD

There are so many notes on the guitar, and so many possibilities of how and where to play them. There are six strings, and somewhere between 20 and 24 frets, depending on your guitar. There are a zillion different methods to map the fretboard.

Here are our favorites:

▶ Map the fretboard using the circle of 4ths

 ADAM: *Here's one that I learned when I was at music school. I had a teacher named Peter Butterfield and he showed us a method that I found very useful. It uses the circle of 4ths.*

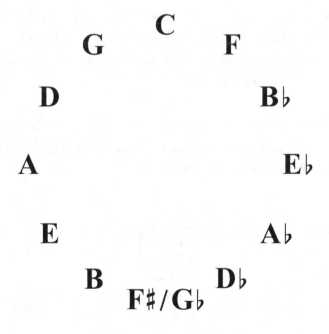

Figure 6. The circle of 4ths.

Pick a single string and take it around the circle starting with *C*. Say each note name out loud as you play it. Doing these two things together builds more pathways between your cerebellum (the part of your brain that controls coordination, timing, and fine motor skills) and your cerebrum (the big boss, in charge of learning, memorizing, and much more). The more connections you build, the more optimally you can perform on any given task.

- Do this with a metronome going. You don't have to play very fast: try letting four "ticks" go by before you play another note.
- Try not to look at the neck too much. If you need to glance for reference that's fine, but try as best you can to keep your eyes forward.
- Repeat this for all six strings.
- Over a period of days, you could set the metronome faster or keep it at the same pace. I like slowly eliminating the time between notes—three "ticks," then two, then one. This can help it feel fluid without straining or rushing into the next note.
- If you spend a week doing this, you will know all of the notes on your neck before long.

You can apply this idea to virtually any piece of musical material. Now let's see how it can translate to memorizing chord shapes. Let's say you just learned this chord:

Figure 7. F chord, open position.

It's an F chord, voiced on the top four strings. The index finger frets two notes at once. You could call this a mini barre chord.

The root is on the 4th string, and it's also on the 1st string. You could follow either string around the circle of 4ths, maintaining the same chord form. As you do that, see those notes that you've spent the last week or so finding? Now we're taking these notes and voicing chords around them. If you need to play, say, a C♯ chord—no problem. You find a movable chord shape like this one and relocate your 4th string root to the 11th fret.

You can certainly do this for more advanced chord voicings. The process is the same: find your root note, and locate that note on the fretboard while your other fingers keep the chord form.

If you want to play a rootless voicing, this still works. In that case, pick any note in the voicing from which you can clearly understand/hear its relationship to the root—the 3rd, for instance. Then locate the chord you are after in the same way.

▶ To recap:

- Map the fretboard using the circle of 4ths.
- Practice on your guitar, and away from the guitar (see chapter 4, "Practice Without Your Guitar").
- Make a map in your mind. Be able to visualize it, even with your eyes closed, and you'll never be lost again.

ETHAN: *You can also apply Adam's circle-of-4ths approach to intervals and octave shapes. I think for every note you know on the guitar, you should also be able to find the other notes around it that are easily fingered.*

Many "straight-ahead" styles of guitar playing have moves or ideas that are based on two-note shapes (a.k.a. double-stops) in 3rds, 4ths, 5ths, 6ths, and octaves. A great number of creative guitarists have tapped into the power of 2nds and 7ths (as well as all of the above) to create sonorities that confound the ear but are fairly easy to play. In other words, there's something for everyone here!

▸ Mapping intervals

An interval is the distance from one note to another. In this context, we play a root note and find as many intervals above and below it as we can, fretboard location permitting. For right now, let's set our root note up as the E on the 7th fret of the 5th string:

ASCENDING
- Minor 2nd: same string, one fret up/one string over, four frets back
- Major 2nd: same string, two frets up/one string over, three frets back
- Minor 3rd: same string, three frets up/one string over, two frets back
- Major 3rd: same string, four frets up/one string over, one fret back
- Perfect 4th: one string over, same fret
- Tritone: one string over, one fret up

- Perfect 5th: one string over, two frets up
- Minor 6th: one string over, three frets up/two strings over, two frets back
- Major 6th: two strings over, one fret back
- Minor 7th: two strings over, same fret
- Major 7th: two strings over, one fret up
- Octave: two strings over, two frets up

Why not descending? We could list the descending intervals (played below the root, instead of above), but they're a lot more contingent upon which string your root is played on.

For example: if your root note is on the 3rd fret of the high E string, almost every note played against it in position is a descending interval, except for the other intervals also on the high E string. However, if your root note is on the 3rd fret of the low E string, only the 2nd fret, 1st fret, and open string are available for descending intervals. You can't play them at the same time because they're on the same string. Strings like D and G have equal ascending and descending intervals on both sides. Why didn't we use one of those as an example? Read on...

▶ Giant steps

If you keep going past an octave, you'll find even wider intervals—9ths, 10ths, 11ths, 13ths. 12ths and 14ths exist, but the extra octave jump doesn't make them sound any less like a 4th or 7th. The widest interval that those of us without extendable 4th fingers can comfortably grab while still holding down the root is a major 13th: four strings over, two frets up.

▶ Finger tips

You'll change your left-hand fingering as the intervals require. If you need to play an interval that's one fret back, fret the root with your 2nd finger. If the interval is two frets back, fret the root with your 3rd finger. Three or four frets back, fret the root with your 4th finger. For all the other intervals, your 1st finger will fret the root, and the other note will be fretted according to 4th fret positioning (see Tip "Position Yourself" on page [43]).

▶ The B string

The major 3rd interval that's created by the tuning of the G and B strings puts a bit of a kink in things. The guitar is tuned almost all the way in intervals of 4ths. In other words, almost every string is tuned a perfect 4th interval above the previous one (remember the circle of 4ths? Yeah, that thing). *Except* from strings G to B. That's a major 3rd: one interval narrower than a 4th.

"Why the heck did they do that?" you may ask. *"Why make guitar more complicated than it already is?!"*

It might have something to do with enabling the highest and lowest strings to be the same note, which makes open chord shapes a lot more possible. Some people tune their guitar to perfect 4ths all the way across so that all the shapes are symmetrical, but we don't think that brings you any closer to making good music. It's a personal choice.

So, any interval or octave fingering that involves the B string in any way, whether you play it or skip past it, will require you to put your non-root note one fret *higher* than you normally would. Keep that in mind as you're playing through intervals.

▶ Practice strategy

What if you were to work out all of the intervals available off any root note on any spot on the guitar? You can! Pick one root per day. There are six strings, and 12 easily accessible frets. That's 72 days, with one root note per day. It would take around 10 weeks—a good medium-term project, and we're sure you'll know some stuff you didn't before. Hang up a picture of a fretboard in your practice space, and check off a fret once you've played through its neighboring intervals.

Don't worry about memorizing the locations (which string, which fret, etc.) as they relate to a particular root note. The idea is to internalize the interval shapes so that you can hear and play the sound regardless of where it is on the guitar.

▶ Bonus: octaves

Octaves are such an important part of guitar vocabulary that it's helpful to see where they're all located. They can help you connect fretboard positions and are beautiful sounds on their own (check out Wes Montgomery and George Benson). Here are some different octave fingerings as they relate to the root note being on specific strings:

- Root on 6: two strings over, two frets up/three strings over, three frets back
- Root on 5: two strings over, two frets up/three strings over, two frets back
- Root on 4: two strings over, three frets up/three strings over, two frets back
- Root on 3: two strings over, three frets up

This is a good illustration of how the major 3rd between G and B affects the changing of the shapes as you move across the strings.

PART III: REFLECTIONS

If the "Challenges" section was big picture, "Reflections" is the ultra-wide, zoomed-out big picture. This section is a mix of lessons learned from real-life experience, music we think you should check out, and musings on how to navigate the seeming infinitude of being a guitarist in today's world. This is the part of the book to read when you're thinking about why you're doing what you're doing, and what you'd like to do next. Play on!

CHAPTER 12:

IS BEING "GOOD" ACTUALLY GOOD?

REFLECTION: What Makes a Good Guitarist?

A Tipster (a viewer of *Guitar Tips*) writes: *Hi Adam and Ethan. I've been playing guitar for years and years. I practice every day and on weekends for hours—anywhere from two per day during the week and four to eight per day on weekends. How can I tell if I am good?*

How can *any of us* tell if we are good? Context matters. We all have different goals, whether they're written down on a list or not—a list helps, though. A very broad definition of a "good guitarist," without considering style, professionalism, or career aspirations, is as follows: *a good guitarist makes real music, reliably.* That doesn't mean being perfect and bulletproof at all times. Everybody has good days and bad days, but for the most part, a good guitarist is solid at the things they're solid at.

Quantity of practice isn't all that important. Getting the quality right of what you're doing is the first and most important step. Once that's on track, then you can adjust the quantity depending on your goals and your life.

Being a good guitarist has almost nothing to do with statistics and checklists. It's great to know the Dorian mode all over the neck and play challenging pieces of music at impressive tempos, but it's not a requirement. That said, here are some things you can work on to become your own version of a "good guitarist":

1. **Be able to reliably tune a guitar without a tuner**
   We have tuners and use them, but you might end up at a gig without a tuner and need to tune by ear. Perfect pitch

is not necessary (you don't have to be exactly at A440), but what you do need is a frame of reference, be it a pitch pipe or tuning fork or another instrument. You're just trying to get the guitar in tune with it itself and any other instruments you're playing with.

2. **Reliably play in time, with or without a metronome**
   In our teaching, we often come across people who have gotten really good at playing the guitar, but their sense of time is not that strong. You need to be able to play with a metronome because it requires similar skills as playing with other people. Other musicians' sense of time may not be so predictable, but at least you're synchronizing with an external time source. Also, many recording sessions nowadays do require playing to a click track (essentially a metronome). Turn the click off, too, and record yourself playing what feels like "in time" to you, and listen back. Does it feel like you're playing in time when you listen back? If not, work on that.

3. **Play a melody in different keys and different octaves.**
   Move around the fretboard without counting the dots or getting out a tape measure

4. **Play many songs in any area of music you care about**
   It's one thing to say you're a bossa nova guitarist because you happen to like bossa nova, but do you know the songs from the repertoire? Could you go to a bossa nova jam session and hang in there? If you can play the essential elements of the song without charts, without a fakebook or iPad, beginning to end, in time, then you know the song.

5. **Become familiar with the iconic guitarists in the music you care about**

Who are the players you need to know? Why are they important? What are some of the elements of their style? If you're
into a specific style of music, you should also know some of the
lesser-known players. If you tell me you're into electric blues,
I may ask, "Who are you into?" If you tell me B.B. King and
Stevie Ray Vaughan, that's great. Those are seminal players,
no doubt. But what about Otis Rush, Little Milton, or Lowell
Fulson? There are *lots* of people you can check out that may
not be the first names that come to mind. Check out as much
as you can—the iconic players and some of the lesser-known
players. You can learn so much by checking out and learning
from the people that not everyone is imitating.

6. **Play along with recordings**
   You like electric blues? Put on a record and play along. Can
   you work out some of what's already being played? Can you
   make up your own parts on the spot that fit in with what's
   happening? Even though the music may already be complete,
   can you find some other thing to add to it? It can be something
   small and simple. That's much like what you'll be doing on a
   gig: listening to what's happening and adding something that
   makes the music better.

7. **Take responsibility for your own growth**
   Look at where you are, look at where you want to be, and
   think about how you want to get there. That might mean
   seeking out a teacher or buying a book to study. It might mean
   organizing your practice time more effectively.

8. **Be a part of your community**
   Even if you're onstage by yourself, having a community of
   like-minded people will inspire you, challenge you, and help
   you grow. Find those people. They may be guitarists, they may

be other instrumentalists and vocalists. They might not even be musicians—as long as they're people whose "thing" you're excited about and want to support.

Being a good guitarist doesn't require you to develop a distinctive voice on the instrument. It's wonderful to be interested in the guitar and interested in doing something fresh, but if you're interested in working, that's great too. If you want to play in a pit orchestra on Broadway, you don't need to develop a unique voice—you're there to play what's on the page and to do it to the best of your abilities. If you're in a Rolling Stones cover band, you're doing your best to sound like Keith Richards or Ron Wood (or Brian Jones or Mick Taylor). Judging whether you're a good guitarist depends largely on your own goals.

REFLECTION: Eclecticism vs. Specialization

A Tipster wrote: *Should I focus on one style and learn everything I can about it, or should I try to study all the styles?*

This is a hard question to answer. Everybody learns differently, and everybody lives differently. Specialization can be a rewarding way to go: get really great at a particular thing you're into by working hard at it for five years, ten years, or even longer. At that point, your knowledge and your musical acumen may be one of a kind.

You've got to make a living in the meantime, obviously. For some people, gigging *is* the living, so maybe you have to join the cover band that keeps you working regularly or play show tunes on a cruise ship or whatever. Look, if people are paying you money to play the guitar, that is really cool! If it happens to be away from the thing you're most interested in creatively, do your best to be professional about it. *Do good work.* In your own time, keep studying the thing that turns you on.

The risk with learning one style is that it may limit the gigs you get. If you're an expert at, say, Django Reinhardt-style swing guitar, people may not think of you for their blues-rock cover band that's working five nights a week. If you're a more well-rounded player, on the other hand, you may never be the greatest at any one thing, but you may be more employable.

After five or ten years of studying one area of music, you might want to take on a different style. Let's say you've become an expert on gypsy swing and then you decide to learn classical guitar. They have different techniques, repertoire, instrument, nail care—different *everything*. It's not going to be easy, but at least you're coming to it after having a guitar in your hands for thousands of hours and playing some actual gigs. In all that time, you will have grown as a person as well. You've set yourself up to make quicker progress at any new style, despite the differences.

Everything doesn't have to happen right now. You can work hard at one thing for a long time while planning ahead, thinking about what you want to do with your next wave of growth.

ETHAN: *I think choosing to specialize or learn a variety of styles depends on the future you imagine for yourself, regardless of whether your instrument earns you a living. Do you get excited about the idea of doing something completely different from one day (or week) to the next? Or does it satisfy you more to chip away at one thing and see how far down the rabbit hole you can go?*

There are few, if any, absolute musts that encompass the infinite possibilities of the guitar, besides "don't hurt yourself!"* Principles of technique, practice approaches, and repertoire come into play when you decide what type of music you want to play and when you make a clear choice about what's important to you.

These days, virtually the entire history of recorded music is at our fingertips, immediately accessible. It can feel paralyzing (where do I start?!), but it's also empowering. The growing musician now has the opportunity to curate their own set of values and create their own tradition from a limitless palette, right from the beginning of their musical journey. So, the choice you make about what you want to play can be entirely personal, and if you're in

---

* I was going to include "play in tune" as well, but Arto Lindsay threw that one out the window in 1978. If you haven't heard Lindsay, put down this book and go listen to his band DNA and the first Lounge Lizards album. (You're welcome.)

a musical community and making your work heard, chances are other musicians will dig your individuality—they may even see a place for it in their music.

Another thing to consider: deeply immersing yourself in one style doesn't mean shutting yourself off to any other music outside of what you're studying. All the great musicians I've ever known love a wide and diverse variety of music, even if it sounds nothing like the music they themselves play.

A lot of so-called "specialists" are a lot more eclectic than you might think, and it's often incredibly illuminating to hear how a great musician in one idiom sounds when placed outside of the zone you most often hear them in. (Ever heard Norman Blake play "Sweet Georgia Brown"?)

So, follow your curiosity. Learn what you love, until you get sick of it. Then learn something else you love.

REFLECTION: Thinking About Thinking

One of the most common questions asked of improvising musicians is, *"What are you thinking about when you're playing?"* Let's start by listing some thoughts we don't have (or at least try not to) when we're playing or performing:

- *"Okay, the chord is D-7, the Dorian mode goes good with D minor 7, now I'll play D Dorian in 7th position, starting on the G string."*
- *"Look out for that chromatic ii-V-I you always miss!"*
- *"Down-up-down-up-down-up-down-up..."*

Mid-play, be it onstage or anywhere else, is not the time to be thinking about music in such a mechanical sense. It's like trying to solve a puzzle in the middle of a song, which will have you constantly playing catch-up to everything that's happening around you. That's a reactive state, and while it's good to be reactive to your fellow musicians, you also want to be proactive—instigating your own ideas and bringing your unique self to the music. As real as the mechanics of music may be, it's better to save your analysis for the practice room.

When you're on stage, you have bigger concerns:

- Flow
- Keeping the ideas moving forward
- Connecting with the other people you're playing with
- Connecting with the audience you're playing for

In the moment, you may end up playing plenty of stuff that's impractically fingered or doesn't follow a particular picking scheme—and that's okay. *Going for it is good.*

Some people have said it's best not to think about anything at all while you're playing. Like anything else, it takes practice. If you can't stop yourself from thinking, here are a few prompts to help you get out of your head:

- Pick a word and play musical ideas that describe that word. Don't use musical words, like *diminished* or *pentatonic*, but descriptive, colorful language like *blue, staggered, concrete.*
- Play in opposites: try four bars in one mood, and four bars in another. This could happen in a static harmonic setting (i.e., one or two chords) or in a song form.
- Set a limitation. Play a whole chorus of blues in one octave. Restrict yourself to any pair of strings. Play a particular interval—and only that interval. Hit the 9 on every chord...you get the idea.
- Play a phrase—literally. Think of a few words, and speak them in your head, over and over. Play the rhythm that you're "speaking."

Playing these games gives you specific goals to move toward, but they're different from goals that relate to playing the "right" scale, arpeggio, or lick. Consider the way a non-musician thinks about music—the hip Mixolydian stuff is odious. A typical audience member, who's not a trained musician, is going to talk about how a performance made them feel, or describe it in terms of its contours and narrative.

Keep that in mind as you move your own music forward. You can always go back to thinking about music in a nuts-and-bolts way. The truth is, if you already know that stuff, it's probably not going to go away.

CHAPTER 13:
THE REAL WORLD

REFLECTION: Studio Strategies

A Tipster wrote: *I'm interested in how you navigate recording sessions. Specifically, the topic of being directed and produced, and interpreting the criticism, feedback, and direction that you receive from the artist or producer on the job in real time.*

Working as a studio guitar player requires two main skill sets. First of all, creativity. Studio musicians should be able to make something up on the spot when presented with a chart or demo. Can you find something to do on the guitar that adds a new dimension to what's already there?

The second critical element is having a thick skin! You need to be able to keep your head on straight and respond in good humor when confronted with direction, feedback, or criticism.

▶ Book recommendations to help develop creativity and a thick skin!

These books are about mindset—how you are when you arrive at the point of music-making and how you can be as you go forward:

- *The Inner Game of Tennis*, W. Timothy Gallwey
- *Effortless Mastery*, Kenny Werner
- *The Music Lesson*, Victor Wooten

▶ Things you'll never hear in a recording session:

"Hey, could you play the 2nd inversion on the 3rd string set?"
"Could you play the Dorian mode here?"
"Would you try alternate picking instead of economy picking?"

The stuff we might be working on in our practice is not the language spoken in studios. Much more often, the feedback you're given is in layman's terms, or in general creative language ("Make it sound more X," or "less Y"), and it's our job to interpret that into musical decisions.

▶ Get familiar with feedback that's not coming from a guitarist's perspective

If you want to practice this, there are plenty of "creativity prompts" to be found that deal in general terms, not limited to a specific idiom or discipline. Here are a few that have helped us out over the years:

• *Steal Like an Artist*, Austin Kleon
• *What It Is*, Lynda Barry
• *The Artist's Way*, Julia Cameron
• *Oblique Strategies**, Brian Eno and Peter Schmidt

---

* *Oblique Strategies* is a deck of "100 worthwhile dilemmas." For example, one says "*Overtly resist change.*" Say you're practicing improvising over a four-chord progression: you play an idea, where you might think, "*Oh, it's time to change, it's boring.*" Instead, you'd follow what the card says, and resist, trying *not* to change in the place where you think it might be natural to change, rather continuing whatever it is that you're doing.

These are the kinds of things you want to practice because if you're just practicing "guitar stuff," you may get farther away from the kind of feedback you'd get in the studio.

▶ Raise the stakes

Practice producing with a friend. Ideally someone you can get in a room with. Make a simple track, and try producing each other. Apply pressure of some sort—a time limit (30 minutes? One hour?) or money ($50?).

It can be playful, but you want to set a little fire under yourself to give yourself some accountability, to make it more real.

REFLECTION: Eight Lessons from Eight Sessions

Recording yourself and listening back provides a tremendous and rapid opportunity for growth—it doesn't matter if you're recording your own music or someone else's, or if you're recording on your iPhone, in a big-budget studio, or anything in between. When we record, we learn about our sound, our feel, how we fit into an ensemble, and how to best serve the music. We can carry each lesson we learn at a recording session into the future.

 ETHAN: *Adam has played on a lot of records—his own and other people's. Some you have probably heard, and some you haven't. Early on in the process of writing this book, we passed prompts back and forth to each other to generate material.*

Here's one I sent to him: Make a list of several records you've made as a leader or sideman. What's at least one thing you learned from each session that you've carried into your work and practice? Here's what he had to say:

▶ Tracy Chapman—*New Beginning*, 1995

 ADAM: *This was one of my first "real" recording sessions. I'd never worked with a major artist before, or with an experienced producer, like Don Gehman who produced this record. I had also never done business with a major management company. Chapman was with Gold Mountain Entertainment (GME) at the time.*

The financials of this session weren't settled beforehand. We were seven or eight days into a ten-day session before the band received our contracts. GME offered a reasonable deal, and everything worked out in the end, but it was stressful to be working for a whole week without knowing how much money was on the table.

LESSON 1: Whether it's a recording session or any other type of gig, *always* be clear about the money before you start the work.

▶ Trevor Dunn's Trio Convulsant— *Debutantes & Centipedes*, 1999

 ADAM: *Trevor Dunn is a bassist and composer. He wrote an album's worth of instrumental pieces and hired me and drummer Kenny Wollesen to record it with him. Before he sent me any of his music to check out, he gave me a cassette tape to listen to.*

On Side A was Slayer's *Reign in Blood*; on Side B was an assortment of Melvins songs. The guitar tones were super heavy on both sides. I had no idea how to make my guitar sound like that. My rig at that time was a Gibson ES-335 and a Fender Vibrolux, with one pedal—a Bixonic Expandora distortion/fuzz. I thought that a Marshall amp could be the right tool for the job, but I didn't own one and had no idea how to set the controls on an amp like that.

Long story short, I borrowed a Marshall JMP-1 preamp from a friend and asked him for a tutorial. When I listen to that CD now, I'm not sure I ever nailed the Slayer tone, but I did manage to sound authentically heavy while still sounding like myself.

LESSON 2: If you're not sure how to do something, you probably know someone who knows. Ask for help.

▸ **Adam Levy—*Buttermilk Channel*, 2001**

ADAM: *This is a trio record I made with organist Larry Goldings and drummer Kenny Wollesen. We had set aside one studio day (all I could afford at the time) for recording. We started tracking in the late morning and worked until 5:30 p.m. or 6:00 p.m. I felt we'd gotten great takes of all of the tunes, and I was happy that we were wrapping up on the early side. We decided we'd take a short dinner break, then come back and listen to everything we'd recorded.*

Just before we left, I heard the recording engineer gasp—not a sound you ever want to hear.

Due to a technical gaffe that I can no longer recall (a bussing issue on the console, I think), our entire day's work was effectively unmixable. The studio manager tried to make things right by offering us free recording time on another day, but both Goldings and Wollesen were leaving town the next day and would be gone for the foreseeable future. Rescheduling wasn't a promising option.

If I wanted this record to get made, we'd have to come back to the studio after dinner and rerecord the entire album. I was frustrated and upset, to say the least, but that's exactly what we did.

LESSON 3: Keep calm and carry on.

▸ Adam Levy—*The Heart Collector*, 2011

 ADAM: *This is a singer-songwriter record, mostly acoustic. Producer Mark Orton left most of the artistic decisions up to me, but he did help me tighten up my songs—especially in the seams between sections. He suggested things like changing the chord at the end of a chorus, so it felt a certain way going into the next verse or repeating an instrumental passage one more time (or one less time) so that its shape was less boxy or predictable.*

At the time, I was too caught up in the words of my songs to consider such details. When I listen to this record now, I really appreciate Orton's tweaks.

LESSON 4: The charm is in the detail.

▸ Anaïs Mitchell—*Young Man in America*, 2012

ADAM: *Bassist/composer Todd Sickafoose produced this record. Sickafoose works differently than many producers. Rather than recording basic tracks first and then piling on the overdubs, he usually prefers to gather a bunch of creative musicians and have them play together, set up with as much isolation as possible. That allows everyone to interact fearlessly, in real time.*

During the mixing process, Sickafoose can mute instruments, as needed, to bring a track into sharper focus.

LESSON 5: Whether tracking band-on-the-floor style—as Sick-afoose does—or via overdubs, playing without hesitation nearly always yields the best results. Trust your instincts and trust the folks you're working with. Get a little lost, get a little found, and don't be afraid of the places in between.

▶ Adam Levy—*Town & Country*, 2014

 ADAM: *For this trio session with organist Larry Goldings and drummer Matt Chamberlain, I brought only two pieces of gear, my 1964 Gibson ES-335 guitar and my '63 Fender Deluxe amp. Although this is the stuff I use most of the time for live shows in bars and small clubs, it doesn't always work in the studio.*

This 335, strung with flat-wound strings, plugged into this brown-era Deluxe—that's a *rich* sound. It can be a little too much for recording sessions when I'm a sideman. It's a little like hiring Pavarotti to sing backing vocals. But this instrumental session was mine to lead, and I wanted the guitar to speak loudly and proudly. One tone, however compelling, is rarely enough to carry a whole record.

To keep things interesting, I changed pickup settings more frequently than I usually do. I turned the amp volume up or down, depending on how much breakup and compression I wanted for the tune at hand. I used the amp's built-in tremolo on some songs. I had the engineer set up tape echo on others, which was printed as we were recording (not added in post-production).

Working this way meant taking more time to dial in my sound before we recorded each song. It was worth it because the varying tones inspired me to play differently.

LESSON 6: Each tune on a record should have a vibe all of its own. It can be easy to forget this sometimes.

▶ Allen Toussaint—*American Tunes*, 2016

ADAM: *I was brought into this project at the last minute. Toussaint and producer Joe Henry had already completed most of the recording that would become* American Tunes. *They had one studio day left and wanted to track two more songs. Henry called me the day before the session and asked if I was available to record Paul Simon's "American Tune" with Toussaint. I was available—and was thrilled, being a long-time Toussaint fan. And, as luck would have it, I already knew that song pretty well.*

When I got to the studio, the arrangement for this song was still undecided. We tried a few different approaches with the full band, but the dynamic arc wasn't feeling quite right. Then Joe suggested that we start with just vocal (Toussaint) and acoustic guitar (me). The bass and drums would come in on the first bridge, about two minutes into the song.

Was I nervous to be recording so sparsely, with no one else to groove with (or hide behind)? Yes! Breath by breath, I was able to calm myself down enough to play "American Tune" the way that it needed to be played.

LESSON 7: Coming into a session, we never know how a song is going to come together. Our guitar part could be the meat, the potatoes, the gravy, or something else altogether. Playing along with records over the years has helped me appreciate how various musical elements work together.

▸ Adam Levy and Jay Bellerose — *Blueberry Blonde,* 2016

ADAM: *This was originally conceived of as a trio record, with myself on vocals and guitars (acoustic and electric), Larry Goldings on organ, and Jay Bellerose on drums. As the recording dates approached, something else came up for Larry and he wasn't going to be available on the days we had booked. I figured that we should postpone the session until he was available. Jay convinced me otherwise.*

He's a fan of spartan recordings, like Sandy Bull's *Fantasias for Guitar and Banjo* (with drummer Billy Higgins) and *Josh White Sings Ballads - Blues.* Jay believed we could make a satisfying record with just three elements—voice, guitar, and drums. In the end, I think we did.

In the absence of the organ, I thought I'd have to play bass lines, chords, and melodies all at the same time, à la Tuck Andress or Charlie Hunter. Since I really can't do that, I had to get comfortable with leaving more space between the notes and the words.

LESSON 8: It's okay to be me and to play the way I play—empty spaces and all.

REFLECTION: Sound Good at a Reasonable Volume

A "reasonable" volume is probably lower than you think. Every guitar player loves the thrill of plugging into an amp and cranking it up. It sounds good and it feels good. Not only do you hear it, but you also feel the vibrations in your body from that much volume. It can bring out a lot of personality in the guitar. You get to hear overtones and details that you don't hear when the amp is quiet, and every little sound is hyped up.

It's fun, but unfortunately, it's not particularly useful in many recording situations or live situations, especially a live situation where there's a PA system.

If you're playing an outdoor gig where there's no microphone on your amp, and the only way for people to hear you is to crank it up, then crank it up. However, when you're playing in a situation with a whole bunch of people on stage where everyone is mic'd up, there will be a front-of-house engineer (FOH for short). They, with all of their faders on the board, can balance each sound and then project it all through the PA in a way that makes sense for whatever the venue is, whether it's a small club, theater, or stadium.

If you're sending out so much volume from your amp that it's starting to fill up the venue without a microphone, that's not a desirable thing. It takes control away from the engineer, and they can't balance the sound in the way they're trying to. At times, engineers and musicians aren't always on the same page, but in a professional situation, you have to take it in good faith that everybody's working to create the best sound for the audience.

With that attitude in mind, just turn down a bit.

 ADAM: *Sometimes I'll face my amp not toward the audience, but toward the side of the stage. That way, if there's a lot of extra sound coming off the amp, it's not going into the house as much.*

The same is true in the recording studio. While it may be exciting to take your favorite amp into the studio and crank it up, that's going to be harder to capture and harder to hear in the final mix, and it may be bleeding into other microphones. That's not necessarily bad, but you want to be intentional if that's what you're doing.

One way you can achieve this in the studio or on stage is with a smaller amp, something like a Fender Princeton Reverb or Fender Deluxe (i.e., an amp with one speaker, not a ton of wattage). Those things can sound great once you put a mic on them, and maybe some compression or EQ. When you send that out to the house mix or put it in a track for recording, it's going to be easy to work with.

Whatever the size of the amp, if the volume is low enough, it's going to be super-duper squeaky-clean. If what's fun for you is a Fender Bassman on 10, a Princeton on 2 is not going to deliver that to you, even if you have it coming back at you through a monitor (or a headphone box, in the studio). You'll need to have something that creates that kind of overdriven tone and response in a box.

 ADAM: *While there are a ton of overdrive and clean boost pedals on the market these days, my box of choice for many years has been a Boss OD-3. I went to Guitar Center one day, years ago, and I saw this huge*

pedalboard of all Boss pedals. This was long before the current "boutique pedal" craze—Boss was all I was thinking about.

I tried everything they make that's in the "overdrive and distortion" family, and I found that for the way I touch the strings and the way I like to hear sound, the OD-3 was the most neutral, and that's what I was looking for. Some pedals will hype-up certain frequencies or subtract others. That's not bad or wrong, but rather a matter of taste. I didn't want to lose any frequencies, and I didn't want to add any either. I wanted it to sound like I just reached over and turned my amp up, but without actually turning my amp up and creating any of the problems that would entail.

I don't use the OD-3 so much as overdrive as "under-drive." In fact, I always keep the Drive set at 0. I set the Level and Tone controls both to 12 o'clock. It seems to be the perfect stompbox to make my guitar sound the same, but slightly bolder.

You don't need to buy any particular pedal, and a pedal may not even be the ultimate solution for you. There are other parts of your "tone chain" that can help. Strings, for example—heavy ones—help hit the amp with a lot of energy. That also helps the amp sound like it's cranked up a little harder, just by virtue of the fact that you're sending more signal into the front end of the chain. Clean boost pedals push the gain of your signal before it goes to your amp, so that it's being driven just a little harder, but not to the point where you start to get breakup.

CHAPTER 14:

DON'T WAIT FOR PERFECT

REFLECTION: Be Good to Yourself

As the great American arena-rock band Journey once so wisely sang:

> Be good to yourself when, nobody else will
> Oh, be good to yourself
> You're walkin' a high wire, caught in a crossfire
> Oh, be good to yourself

We both often encounter guitar students who beat themselves up a lot. We've done it, you've done it, we all do it. Despite our best efforts, sometimes gigs (or other music-related happenings) just don't go the way that we hoped. You can practice, prepare, bring the right gear, and show up on time, and funny stuff still happens.

If you have a bad gig, let it go, and do your best to have a better one next time. Whatever you do, don't tell anybody else about it. If you get off stage and you felt like it didn't go well, absolutely under no circumstances should you say to anybody *"I'm sorry/that didn't go so well/I suck."* It's just chatter in your head, and no one wants to hear it—especially if they enjoyed your performance.

Do your best to ignore it. It is meaningless. If you know in your heart of hearts that there's something you need to work on, go home and work on it!

Of course, it's okay to be a little critical because that critic is the voice that keeps us trying harder, reaching farther, and growing. However, if we can't also appreciate the stuff that sounds good, or the things we played well, then it's going to be difficult to continue being a creative person.

Take some joy in the things you do well. Make a list of them. If you're not sure what you do well, ask the people you play with. They wouldn't be playing with you if they didn't like what you do, and they'd be happy to tell you if you have no idea. If you don't play with other musicians, ask your guitar teacher. If you don't have a guitar teacher, ask somebody who's heard you play. If nobody's heard you play, get out there and play for somebody!

REFLECTION: Want What You Have

It's always exciting to look at new gear. We like new gear, and you probably do, too. It's fun to have everything you want. It's fun to lust after new gear, make a list of all the things you want, and check them off one by one.

Along the way, though, make sure to get the most out of the gear you do have. Maybe you have a guitar that's not the greatest guitar in the world. You feel like it doesn't inspire you to play, so you don't play very much. No matter how many guitars you look at online or buy or borrow, the guitar you have is the guitar you have, so make a commitment to yourself to play every day. If you appreciate what you already own, chances are good that you'll find more music in there than you thought.

There's an element of "fake it till you make it" that applies here. If you don't have the perfect guitar, pretend that you do, and make the most of it. The human imagination is a powerful thing. There's a lot more to be appreciated in what you have—and if you're at it every day, you *will* improve.

For example, if you're recording every day, you're going to learn a lot about where to place the microphone, how to set the preamp and compression, etcetera, just by recording and listening back. The same is true for playing. If you're reading blogs about all that stuff and not doing it yourself, you're not improving, and you're not getting to know your skills and your preferences. Before you go searching for new gear, see if you can come to know the full capabilities of what you have in your possession right now.

REFLECTION: Advice to a Late Bloomer

A Tipster wrote: *I'm 53 years old. I started playing about four years ago. Never played music prior to that. When I went to go buy my first guitar, I literally had to have the sales guy play it for me because I didn't know a single chord. In general, I'm working in mostly a jazz direction. Could you do a Guitar Tip for those of us who got a late start—how to cover the most ground as efficiently as possible? At times there seems to be so much to learn to become a jazz guitarist that I would need to live another lifetime to reach my goals.*

We both feel that way a lot, even though we each started playing guitar at a relatively young age. We would imagine that many other players feel something like that too. Whenever we're new to anything, it can feel like it could take at least one or two lifetimes of work to master it. That being said, it's astonishing what can happen if we show up every day and do some work.

Here's our list of suggestions to encourage (or at least not discourage) other late bloomers. It's a bit jazz-centric, but each point can be applied to almost any style:

1. **Always practice music *in time***
   Get yourself a metronome, a metronome app, or a drum machine. Work on developing honest and reliable timekeeping every time you pick up the guitar. Even if it means practicing slowly at first, it's worth it.

ETHAN: *The great pianist Alan Pasqua told me in a lesson once, "The only difference between us and the masters is that they have better time than we do." I think that applies to every musical idiom—not just jazz.*

2. Play along with records

There's no better way to develop your sense of what good music *feels* like than to play along with records. In the beginning, it may be challenging to find records that you can play along with because so much music will be going by too quickly for you to keep up with. If that's the case, look for records that feature ballads, like the eponymous *John Coltrane and Johnny Hartman,* Jimmy Smith's *Standards* (featuring some of Kenny Burrell's most beautiful work), or Keith Jarrett's *The Melody at Night, with You.*

3. Learn your shell chords well

Shell chords are elemental shapes, containing just the root, 3rd, and 7th (or sometimes the 6th of a chord). You can play root-7-3, low to high, with the root on string 6; or you can play root-3-7, low to high, with the root on string 5. For dominant chords (G7, for instance), lower the 7th one half step. For minor 7th chords (such as Cm7), lower the 3rd and the 7th one half step each. These six shapes (three chord qualities, with root on string 5 or 6) are all you need to get through nearly any jazz tune.

The other chord types you may encounter in jazz are major or minor 6ths (F6 or Fm6, for example) and diminished 7ths (like D°7). For a major 6th, use 6 instead of 7 (it's a whole step lower). For a minor 6th and diminished 7th, use the minor 3 (lowered by one half step) and the major 6 (again, one whole step lower than 7).

Memorizing these shapes in all keys, all over the fretboard, will take you some time. It will be time well spent! Once you know the shells, you can effectively use them as is for accompanying (or "comping"); you can expand them into more colorful sounds by adding extended or altered chord tones; and you can use them as foundation for solo-guitar arrangements.

 ETHAN: *Shameless plug—Adam's written a great book on shell chords (called, what else? Shell Chords) that's worth diving into if this is a skill you need to strengthen.*

4. Learn tunes

Learn songs, then learn some more. And then...more. If you're trying to fast-track your way into jazz, learning tunes is more important than technique or theory. If you're not sure which pieces to learn, consider the context. If you're mostly playing by yourself, then go ahead and learn your favorites. Do you want to "hang" at a local jam session? Go there once to listen, without your guitar, and make a list of the songs you hear. Learn those, and you'll be more prepared when you come back. If you want to play with a particular musician you know, ask them what songs they've been playing lately and learn those.

Learn to sing some tunes, even if you think you're a lousy singer. Sing out loud—like you mean it. When you sing songs, they live in your body and mind in a deeper place than if you merely memorize the chord shapes. *Really do this.*

5. Transpose, transpose, transpose

Once you think you know a song in its original key, play it in other keys. When you can play a tune in any key, without stumbling, then you truly know it.

6. **Listen to jazz**

Listen actively, not just as background music. You can count this as practice! Get a notepad or notebook and take notes on what you hear. What's happening? Who's playing? What instruments are being played, and how do they work together? What's the quality of the sound? Who takes a solo? Who doesn't? What happens behind the solo?

7. **Transcribe**

In jazz, "transcribing" doesn't necessarily mean writing something down. It's another way of saying *learn how to play something that somebody else already played*. Start with simple things you like: composed melodies (they're usually more focused and more repetitive), then improvised phrases (one at a time), and then maybe a short solo. If you don't know where to start, try Chet Baker. He was a singer and trumpet player, and his solos are typically very melodic. Try the trumpet solo on "Time After Time."

Whatever you're learning, begin by singing along with the recording you're learning it from. You'll really know it when you can sing it by yourself without the record playing. This allows you to learn the rhythmic shape of each phrase, which then makes it easier to fill in the actual notes.

Next, apply it to your instrument by singing and playing at the same time. Match the pitch you're singing to the pitch you're playing on the guitar. When you truly know it on your instrument, you'll be able to play it with or without singing along, in steady time. Continue building your skills and your confidence one transcription at a time.

▶ Everything is connected

The materials in this book relate to one another on many different levels. When you're practicing one of these skills, you can also be practicing nearly every other one.

Here's an example: Let's say you've decided to learn "Bye Bye Blackbird." You begin by singing along with the melody from the rendition on Miles Davis's *'Round About Midnight*. When you can sing it without the recording, turn the record off and accompany yourself with shell voicings. (While you're at it, you might as well do this with a metronome ticking on beats on 2 and 4.)

Tired of the key of F and want to transpose it? Crack open Spotify and find a version in another key. Carmen McRae's recording, for example, is in C. Feel like you know the tune well and want to hear what somebody else played on it? Comp along with the Jimmy Smith recording and steal a few lines from Kenny Burrell.

CHAPTER 15:

THREE DUDES TO DIG

REFLECTION: Dig Bach

There's a litany of resources out there about the brilliance of every musical thing Johann Sebastian Bach ever did (original manuscripts, transcribed arrangements, and recordings) and about his life. Bach would be almost 350 years old if he were alive today. Why does his music still matter? It's so rich and pure that to learn and play any of it is a benefit to one's musicality, regardless of what type of music you usually play.

▶ The transcendent genius of the music

Baroque music is often played with particular attention paid to performing in the style that it was intended to be played when it was composed (in the 1600s and early 1700s). Because music-making tools were different back then (employing *just intonation*, for instance), a lot of this music sounds different when we play it using modern-day instruments.

Even though Bach lived during that time period, the magic of his music makes itself clear regardless of the context it's played in. The beauty of its sound and structure transcends idiom, genre, or style.

▶ Counterpoint

Often, what we play on guitar is thought of as either "lead" (single-note lines) or "rhythm" (chords). Counterpoint is the great in-between. It's an approach to playing that's prevalent in the classical guitar tradition, but a rarity elsewhere.

So much of Bach's music is about counterpoint: the interaction between multiple voices sounding simultaneously. Playing pieces like his lute suites is a great way to get used to the sound and feel of counterpoint. You'll have to solve technical problems (e.g., What left-hand fingerings work for you?), balance the voices dynamically, and tackle many other considerations—improving your musicianship along the way.

▸ Vocabulary for improvisation

One of the amazing things about Bach's music is the way he carries melodic phrases and contrapuntal ideas through chord progressions in elegant and sometimes unexpected ways.

If you're interested in improvising, you might be on the hunt for new ideas you can incorporate into your playing, and he's got a lot of them. Do the same thing with a couple of bars of Bach that you might do with an excerpt from a jazz solo: play it in all the keys, forward and backward, all over the fretboard, and then superimpose it into the structure of a song you play a lot.

▸ Building a personal relationship to your instrument

Bach never composed for the six-string guitar. The instrument, as we know it, hadn't been invented yet. While many guitarists have transcribed Bach's music, playing music on an instrument where it doesn't naturally lay requires you to create a personal relationship with every single musical moment, whether it's in regard to left and right-hand fingering or tone production. It's the same muscle that gets flexed when you learn a saxophone or trumpet solo on the guitar. In that context, you have to figure how to adapt instrument-unique articulations like slurs and scoops to frets and strings.

You don't need to be classically trained to get something big out of Bach. He's for everybody. Here are some suggestions for how you can dig Bach, regardless of how well you already know him:

• Watch some videos of Julian Bream playing Bach on YouTube. Listen actively. Follow each voice through its development and conclusion throughout the piece.
• Learn both parts of one of Bach's two-part inventions. Alternately, ask a buddy to learn the other part, then play it together. If you don't have a jam buddy, record yourself playing one part, then play along with it as you play the other part.
• Learn a movement from one of the lute suites. Learn primarily by ear from a recording, as small a chunk as you can handle at a time. If you read music, supplement with a manuscript. Make note of your favorite parts and improvise your own variations.

REFLECTION: Dig Django

French-Romani guitarist Django Reinhardt was one of the first players to essentially spawn his own genre. Though he had many contemporaries, he popularized the "Jazz Manouche" style and is generally viewed today as the player who set the standard for everyone after him.

In our experience as players and teachers, we've seen that while many players appreciate Reinhardt as fans, playing his music is viewed as a bit of a niche activity with not much middle ground—you're either all in or all out.

We all know a semi-accurate factoid or two (*"You know, he only had two fingers!"*), or it's your whole trip. You get a Selmer-style guitar, you play with a super-duper heavy guitar pick, you learn all the Reinhardt songs, maybe you even play with a silk scarf tied around your neck and learn to speak fluent French.

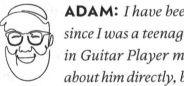 **ADAM:** *I have been a dabbler of Reinhardt's music since I was a teenager. I remember reading about him in Guitar Player magazine—not so much in articles about him directly, but about people he had influenced, like B.B. King and Willie Nelson, who would mention him in interviews.*

Because of that, I would search out whatever I could. Eventually I was able to find an LP of Reinhardt's recordings—a compilation of material from the late 1930s, called Solos/Duets/Trios, Vol. 2. Later on, more music became available, and I got more into it. I wasn't so much into transcribing things note for note, but just absorbing.

In the '90s, I was living in San Francisco and I got to play with a great band called The Hot Club of San Francisco, led by a tremendous guitarist named Paul Mehling. I mostly played rhythm because that was the tradition in Reinhardt's band—there was one lead guitar player and one or two rhythm guitar players. As one of the rhythm guitar players, I had a front-row seat to Paul Mehling's playing and got to learn a lot about the Django Reinhardt style.

You don't have to go full Jazz Manouche obsessive to get a lot of benefits from this music. In fact, Reinhardt is for everybody! Here are a few things to pick up from Reinhardt that you can apply to your own playing, plus a practice strategy for each:

1. **The guitar truly can sing, talk, laugh, and cry**
   Django Reinhardt could play lots and lots of steady eighth notes at all kinds of fast tempos, but that wasn't all he had to offer—far from it.

   A hallmark of his playing is getting a phrase going really quickly, and then suddenly stepping off into something else entirely—one note with a great vibrato, or some little decorative flourish. If you're listening, it holds your attention, keeping you at the edge of your seat with its unpredictability.

   PRACTICE STRATEGY: In your improvisations, aim to create a conversation between one idea and the next.

2. **Old sounds don't have to sound old-fashioned**
   Reinhardt used a lot of diminished chords, augmented chords, and minor 6th chords. To some extent, that's because when he was recording, in the late 1930s and '40s, those were the common harmonies in jazz and popular music.

Also, as mentioned earlier, he really only had good use of his index and middle fingers on his fretting hand: the other two had been damaged in a fire. Apparently, he could use his two damaged fingers for playing octaves and chords, but not much else. So, when you listen to Reinhardt, keep in mind that most of what he's doing is with those two good fingers. A minor 6th chord on the top four strings is easy to get with just two fingers, for example.

Diminished chords are sometimes tossed out in today's world as sounding old-fashioned. These days, if we think of diminished licks, they're most often lumped in with modern jazz vocabulary—wandering and elliptical, angular and chromatic—coming out of players like Allan Holdsworth and Kurt Rosenwinkel.

Reinhardt could play a basic diminished arpeggio, and somehow it never sounds old-fashioned, even listening back today. Go back and reexamine some of these kinds of harmonies and see if there's something in them that you could use in your own vocabulary, even if you don't hear those sounds in the music of today.

PRACTICE STRATEGY: Take a minor 12-bar blues progression and substitute all the minor or minor 7th chords with minor 6th chords. When you improvise, play a minor pentatonic scale, and substitute the b7 with the 6th, a half step down from normal.

3. **Want what you have**
   As far as we know, Reinhardt wasn't sitting around moping and wishing his other two fingers would work better. He just played and played and played. It's so easy for any of us to wish

for things that we don't have instead of going forward with what we do have.

Reinhardt didn't have the advantage that we have in today's world where he could take a survey of all recorded music of all time: he had what he had, he learned what he could from it, and he made it his own. So, don't worry about what you don't have. Take what you do have, get the most out of it, and go forward.

PRACTICE STRATEGY: Try bending into notes with one finger, specifically your first or second finger. Don't limit yourself to Reinhardt-style playing or jazz-related idioms. See what happens when you do it in a blues context, for example.

4. **Learn to love your acoustic guitar**
Some guitarists can fall into a pattern of treating the acoustic guitar like the electric guitar's boring older brother—sonically limiting, less forgiving on the hands, fun in small doses, but not the main event. Listening to Reinhardt puts that presumption to shame.

For most of his career, Reinhardt played acoustic guitar. Near the end of his life, he did record some things on electric, but for the most part, it was all acoustic, with a flat pick. There's so much cool stuff you can do with the acoustic guitar far beyond things that sound like folk music. Reinhardt is the gold standard in that way. He played in a very sophisticated way with a pick on the acoustic guitar, demonstrating that a lack of electrification is no barrier to boundless exploration.

PRACTICE STRATEGY: Give equal practice and playing time to both your acoustic and electric guitar. Play things on your acoustic that you would normally play on electric. You might be surprised by what you hear.

5. **Tunes, beautiful tunes**
Django is credited with over 100 compositions, which is a staggering amount of music considering the relatively short amount of time that he recorded (he passed away at the age of 43).

His compositions are so strong and so rich—melodically, harmonically, and rhythmically—that they transcend style. They don't have to be played like it's 1939. You don't have to play them à la Reinhardt. In fact, you can play them in any style you like!

PRACTICE STRATEGY: Learn three of Django Reinhardt's compositions, and play them with your friends, in any style or setting you like.

▶ Six Essential Reinhardt Tunes:

- "Minor Swing"
- "Swing 42"
- "Nuages"
- "Django's Castle (Manoir de mes Rêves)"
- "Melodie au Crepuscule"
- "Douce Ambiance"

▶ Django Reinhart Recommended Listening:

- *Improvisations 1-5*. Breathtaking solo excursions.
- *Djangologie* Series, Vol. 1-20. The whole enchilada.

REFLECTION: Dig Dawg

Dawg is David Grisman: mandolinist, bandleader, and composer extraordinaire. He's been a living legend in the world of mandolin and bluegrass for over 50 years, but his original music hasn't yet become part of the lingua franca (or common language) of the guitar-playing community beyond the bluegrass world.

Why should you care about Dawg? Why are we writing about a mandolinist in a book of guitar tips? First of all, he's employed a treasure trove of stellar guitarists in his band, and their work with him is essential listening if you're interested in any of them. These include Tony Rice, Mark O'Connor, John Carlini, Frank Vignola, and Grant Gordy, to name a few.

Grisman's musical world is also the perfect meeting point of two very distinct musical idioms. At the risk of sounding like a press release, his musical world seamlessly brings together the folk process behind bluegrass and related acoustic music, with the subtleties of improvised instrumental music, with a deep grounding in both traditions. He's synthesized them into his own sophisticated yet accessible musical language.

He had a major influence on most of today's most acclaimed "genre-busters." If you love players like Julian Lage and Chris Thile, and want to know where they come from, study Dawg. A lot of their approach to making music can be traced back to the model he set in the 1970s and onward.

Grisman is a prolific composer and has written hundreds of tunes. Like Django's music, Grisman's songs are extremely malleable on a textural and stylistic level, always sounding like quality music no matter what setting they're in. The forms are clear, and the melodies are catchy.

His approach to harmony is unique—there aren't any chord changes out of the ordinary per se, but the progressions have this "blocky" quality that seems to come from folk or bluegrass, even when so-called jazz chords are being played (anything beyond a 1-3-5 triad). Everybody improvises on the tune, and usually any vocabulary works. So, dig Dawg—you won't be disappointed!

▸ Six Essential Dawg Tunes:

- "Dawg's Waltz"
- "EMD"
- "16/16"
- "Blue Midnite"
- "Waiting on Vassar"
- "Telluride"

▸ David Grisman Recommended Listening:

- *The David Grisman Quintet.* This is the record that started it all—featuring Tony Rice, Darol Anger, and Todd Philips.
- *Live at the Great American Music Hall 1979.* Slightly after the first DGQ-20 album, all of the above plus Mike Marshall on second mandolin. Absolutely on fire.
- *Quintet '80.* Mark O'Connor replaces Rice, more shredding ensues.

- *Tone Poems.* A duet album with Rice, each track played on a different pair of vintage guitar and mandolin.
- *Del & Dawg Live.* With fellow legend Del McCoury—straight-ahead bluegrass, "brother-duet" style.
- *Dawg Duos.* An eclectic mix of late-'90s duets with musicians of all stripes—Hal Blaine to Edgar Meyer, Denny Zeitlin to Zakir Hussain, plus an 11-year-old Julian Lage's recording debut.

CHAPTER 16:

DON'T STOP

REFLECTION: Forward Ever, Backward Never

Forward ever, backward never, in these three ways:

▶ Keep the song going

One thing we notice when we're working with students is that often they will start on an idea, and if they play a wrong note, they'll completely stop. We've all experienced this. We play a mistake, and suddenly all the chatter in our head takes over—*I'm not a good guitar player, I'm not a good person*, and so on. The hands give up, and our focus is broken.

It takes discipline to keep playing after you've hit a bum note or two. The methodology of how you keep on going is personal, and we encourage you to find your own way that works to motivate yourself to not stop.

Remember, on a real gig—a live performance with live people with other live musicians (or by yourself)—stopping is not allowed. It's not part of "what you can do in music." The more that you include stopping in your practice time, the more you reinforce the possibility that stopping is an option (and it is not an option!).

Another kind of stopping that's closely related is this: you play a wrong note, and then start over in a different area of the neck, figuring *"this area has been stunk up, so I'll go over here and try something new,"* because you want to get as far away from where you stunk up as possible. Instead, sit in your stink for a minute and see if you can make something cool out of it.

▸ Practice in perpetual motion

ADAM: *I remember, years ago, reading about an approach to practicing by guitarist Howard Roberts that he called "Super Chops." It has to do with taking a tune (say, "All the Things You Are") and playing an unbroken stream of eighth notes. This helps you connect the dots, realizing that from any note you can go in any direction and keep moving through the harmony.*

You have to think ahead a little bit because if you're not thinking ahead of where you are, you may paint yourself into a corner—you may run out of string, or run out of fingers, or neck. The point is to not stop, but also to not judge. If you start judging, you're going to start stopping.

You can take it as slowly as you need to, but it doesn't have to be a speed thing. In the actual *Super Chops* book, though, it was. You'd pick a tempo you could do eighth notes comfortably at, and over time you would increase the tempo until it was burning, and you could play steady eighth notes throughout.

This is a good thing to practice, not all the time, but every so often. I wouldn't encourage you to play this way too much of the time on a real gig because it can be taxing on people's ears. Make sure to also practice playing real musical phrases that have clear beginnings, middles, and ends—phrases that have a shape to them.

There's lots of Bach music that works like this (the partitas and sonatas for solo violin, for example). More guitaristically, Joe Pass's instructional books have lots of 12-bar blues lines that just go, and go, and go, and go.

Practicing moving forward in a perpetual motion of eighth notes is good for your technique, good for your ears, and good for your imagination.

▶ Don't give up

Everybody has tough weeks, tough months, tough years, tough periods in their life. If you love music, find a way to keep doing it.

Country music legend Johnny Cash was once interviewed by Terry Gross for the radio show *Fresh Air*. In their conversation, Cash told Gross about a period before he made his final few records, when he felt he was drifting. He wasn't selling many records, and his record label wasn't being supportive. It'd be easy to see how somebody in that position would just give up, but Cash wanted to keep making records and doing what he loved to do. Then he happened to meet Rick Rubin, which led to a signing with American Recordings, and he went on to make some of the best music he'd ever made.

It's hard to see around the corner when you're having a dark episode of an hour, a day, a week, a month, or a year. If music is important to you and it brings you joy, find a way to keep doing it. If your goal is to have a life full of music, don't stop.

REFLECTION: Five Ways to Keep Growing

▶ Set clear goals

Take the time to set clear creative goals: What do you want to make? Be really specific about it.

If you're making a go of a career in music, have clear career goals. Think about where you want to be in the world of music, professionally. Who are the people that you want to align yourself with? What are the important markers for you?

Write down these goals, and look at that piece of paper every day to remind yourself exactly what you're working toward and how the things you're doing today are going to help you get there. There may be detours and potholes along the way, but the clearer you are in your own mind about why you're doing what you're doing, the more diversions you can avoid, and the more directly you can get where you're trying to go.

▶ Take stock

If you have some earlier recordings of yourself—a record you made last year, or a show you played two years ago, or a rehearsal from a month ago—listen to what you sounded like in the past.

Also listen to what you sound like now. If you don't have a recent recording, make one. It can be as simple as practicing alone or rehearsing with a group. Maybe invite some friends over, play a show just for them, and record that. Whatever you're able to record, listen back and be honest with yourself. See what's going on there. Looking back, are you going in a good direction? If you're not, try to steer your ship in the direction you want to go. If you're not clear about which direction that is, revisit setting goals.

▸ Play with musicians who are better than you

Whenever possible, play with musicians who challenge you. It kicks your ass in the best way. That's not easy for everyone. You may not know where to find those people, or you may feel intimidated to initiate a conversation with them (let alone suggest getting together to play). In any case, try to make it happen—you will learn so much by playing with people who are better than you.

They may give you some advice, or they may not say anything at all. Sometimes you play with musicians who are on a higher level, and they don't want to teach you—they just want to play the music! Either way, it's on you to pay attention and get the lessons, both spoken and unspoken.

Side note: Make sure you pay that forward later. When you find yourself further down the road, and some younger, less experienced musician reaches out to you, make yourself available.

▶ Eat your vegetables

Literally and figuratively. First and foremost, take care of your health: eat well, exercise, get a good night's sleep, drink plenty of water. You're going to need your body as you grow as a musician: there won't be much point to growing creatively if your body is falling apart.

On the musical side, remember that practice time shouldn't be spent playing the same songs you know and the same licks you know. Practice things that will push you in the direction of your goals. That may mean you're practicing stuff that isn't fun or doesn't sound good today. It may not sound good tomorrow or next week either, but keep practicing until it does start to sound good. Ideas become real music by developing control in your hands and clarity in your mind.

▶ Push yourself past your comfort zone

We all have things that we tell ourselves are beyond our limitations. Once per week (at least), push yourself past that boundary line, even if it's just one or two small steps. That's how you grow. You take a gig you're not quite ready for, you take up a new instrument, you sing onstage, etc.

REFLECTION: You Are What You Practice

Someone once said that doing the same thing over and over again and expecting different results is the very definition of insanity.* We can apply this to our guitar practice. Ask yourself these questions: What exactly are you trying to achieve on the instrument? Where would you like to be, as a guitarist, one year from today?

Once you've got a clear picture in mind, ask yourself: What are the specific things you can practice to get yourself there? Make a list, as short or as long as you like. Then, for the next year, practice those things and eliminate everything else from your daily routine.

Examples:

• If you want to get better at playing grooves, work hard on your groove playing. This may mean that you don't worry about studying harmony or melody for a while.
• If you want to be a stronger soloist, practice soloing. For instance, you could craft some 8-bar or 16-bar solos—with clear beginnings, middles, and endings—over the kinds of chord progressions you'd like to be fluent with. This may mean that you don't worry about practicing chords for a while.
• If you want to develop your ears, focus your study time on ear training. This may mean that you don't worry about practicing technique for a while.

---

* Although this wise notion has been attributed to Albert Einstein, Benjamin Franklin, and others, no evidence definitively links it to any particular smartypants.

One year from now, you may find that you still have work to do. In fact, we can almost guarantee that. However, we can also guarantee you'll be a lot closer to reaching your goals.

If you fall back into the same old practice routines instead, you'll be more or less the same guitarist you are today, only one year older.

Insane, right?

THIS IS THE END— AND IT ISN'T

If you're reading this, you've reached the end of *String Theories*. Whether you've wrung every page for all its worth or skimmed lightly, we hope that you've found some things in this book that will benefit you today and in all of your tomorrows. We aimed to share ideas and activities that you can do now and that you can revisit later, as you continue to grow. Musical growth is the big idea, after all.

If you've bought a physical edition of *String Theories*, we encourage you to make it your own. Inscribe your name in it and the date you bought it. Write your thoughts or feelings in the margins as they occur to you. Highlight, underline, cross out, doodle. Getting personal with these pages may help you feel more invested in the material here—which, in turn, will get you more invested in your practice time. The more energy you put into the hours of action and reflection, the more you'll get out of it.

Dig you.

ABOUT THE
AUTHORS

▸ Adam Levy

 Adam Levy is a storied guitarist, composer, and songwriter with several original albums to his credit, including *Buttermilk Channel* (with organist Larry Goldings and drummer Kenny Wollesen) and *Blueberry Blonde* (with drummer Jay Bellerose). He has been featured on recordings by Norah Jones, Tracy Chapman, Joe Henry, Allen Toussaint, Vulfpeck, and other esteemed artists. As a sideman, Levy has traveled the world playing alongside singer/songwriters such as Lisa Loeb, Rosanne Cash, and Lizz Wright, and has performed his own music on in innumerable stages as well. He has taught at the University of Southern California, Los Angeles College of Music, and New York University. He is the author of *Play the Right Stuff* as well as six TrueFire guitar courses,

and he hosts the series *Guitar Tips Pro* on Patreon. Levy currently lives in New York City, where he leads the Mint Imperials (a trio with bassist Andy Hess and drummer Tony Mason) and co-leads a quartet with pedal-steel guitarist Rich Hinman.

Learn more at adamlevy.com.

▶ Ethan Sherman

 Ethan Sherman is a guitarist and composer known for moving between a wide variety of musical worlds with uncommon ease and a deeply personal sound. He's released numerous albums of original music, most recently *Indoor Vistas.* As a sideman, he's recorded and performed around his home of Los Angeles with artists as diverse as Nels Cline, Harrison Whitford, Patrick Shiroishi, Sean & Sara Watkins, Lou Roy, Johanna Samuels, and Ed Helms. He is currently touring with Michael Bublé. *The Fretboard Journal* called him "one of those rare individuals who can hold his own playing electric or in traditional bluegrass setting." Sherman resides in Los Angeles, where he performs, records, and teaches privately.

Learn more at ethanshermanmusic.com.